RAILROADS OF DELMARVA

RAILROADS OF DELMARVA

A PICTORIAL HISTORY

DOUGLAS POORE

FONTHILL

Fonthill Media Inc.
www.fonthillmedia.com
office@fonthillmedia.com

First published 2020

ISBN 978-1-63499-218-3

Typeset in Mrs Eaves XL Serif Narrow
Printed and bound in England

CONTENTS

Acknowledgments

The first person I have to thank is Samuel Harrington. Without his belief in the railroad, I would have never grown up with a rail line in my backyard and my early lover affair with the iron horse may never have happened.

To all the train buffs that inspired and aided me: Jim Bowden, Keith Short, Ed Kline, Chase Andrews, Royden Powell, Joe Walder, Richard Layne, John Conley and so many more. May each of you get the highball signal on your road of life.

To John Hayman, the author of the "bible" of the railroad industry of Delmarva. Thank you for your research that set up my success and for your encouragement.

To my travel partner, railroad spotter, and newly christened rail nut, my wife, Lisa: I love you.

To Kena and the rest of the Fonthill staff, thank you all for the guidance and encouragement.

To all the museums, historical societies, Facebook group members and anyone else that provided photos and stories for this book, thank you. A special thank you to the Greater Harrington Historical Society. Any photo not marked is courtesy of this organization.

To all that read this book: Never lose the romance of the railroads. Follow your true north.

Introduction

The railroad. The iron horse. One of the great achievements of the Industrial Revolution. Since the 1830s, the world has had a never-ending love affair with the railroad. Even today, railroads are utilized by countries to move the biggest percentage of their freight from point to point and in most countries, it is the leading mode of mass transportation.

In its early years, people doubted the railroads. But as they grew, so did our affection for them. Stories of romance, intrigue, robber barons, and men with curly mustaches tying the helpless maiden to the tracks fueled our growing infatuation. In fact, the first movie ever made was a 50-second silent film about an arriving passenger train. From there, the legends grew. Stories about men working on the train such as John Henry, who was an African American folk hero, were turned into songs. Countless other folk tales and songs from America's rich past have the railroad as their focus or backdrop. Movies such as the *Harvey Girls*, *Murder on the Orient Express*, and even more recent movies, such as *The Polar Express*, have all used the train to tell their story. The train has even made its presence felt during the holiday season. Many homes, even today, have a train running around the Christmas tree.

As much as the railroad has become a part of America in ways we never imagined, it still at its heart is used today much the same way it was in its early days, to move people and freight. The American Civil War proved what a vital link the railroad would become in times of war. So much so, that even that conflict had stories specifically based on escapades of the railway. In World War I and World War II, the railroad was both a vital link and a major target of the armies. Everyone knew the vital importance the railroads had now become. After those conflicts, America turned to a love affair with the automobile, but even today a larger portion of cargo moves by rail than any other method. While in other countries, people would not be able to travel without the passenger train, as it is the main stay of their mass transit system.

Delaware had one of the earliest railroads to ever be constructed, The New Castle and Frenchtown in 1835. And even for a small region, the Delmarva Peninsula saw no less than forty-plus railroads incorporated and running through its history. Most where short line railroads that ran from point to point carrying passengers and freight alike. Traveling from major ports and cities, these rail lines opened up the region. Prior to the railroad coming in the 1850s, growth in all three states that make up this area—Delaware, the Eastern Shore of Maryland, and the Eastern Shore of Virginia—had all but stalled.

By the 1940s, almost the entire Delmarva Peninsula was under the control of the mighty Pennsylvania Railroad. They had slowly acquired all the short lines that crisscrossed the area. With those changes came closing of certain lines and changes to many others. As the railroad industry floundered and eventually collapsed, Conrail was created by the federal government to rebuild this vital and once flourishing industry. In 1997, most of Conrail was sold to Norfolk Southern and CSX, completing the return of the railroads in the area to private control, a process which began in 1987. Not only have we seen the return of major railroad corporations to the area, but in more recent times the short line railroad companies, those that once dominated the Delmarva Peninsula, have returned and are once more vital to the success of the railroad industry.

Certainly the railroading history of Delmarva lacks the glamour of the famous trains such as the Broadway Limited, the Super Chief, and the Orange Blossom Special to name a few, but there are still famous lines and stories that have existed since the first train in the 1830s. This book highlights some of the scenes of railroading on Delmarva from that time to current day. While not an in-depth history, I hope this book will, through its photos, tell the story of one area's rich railroading traditions.

The New Castle and Frenchtown Rail Road began as a turnpike, incorporated in Maryland in 1810 and in Delaware in 1811. The road connected steamship landings in Maryland and Delaware. In 1830, both states changed the charters to permit a railroad being built along the trail. The railroad was completed in February 1832. [*Courtesy of the New Castle County Historical Society*]

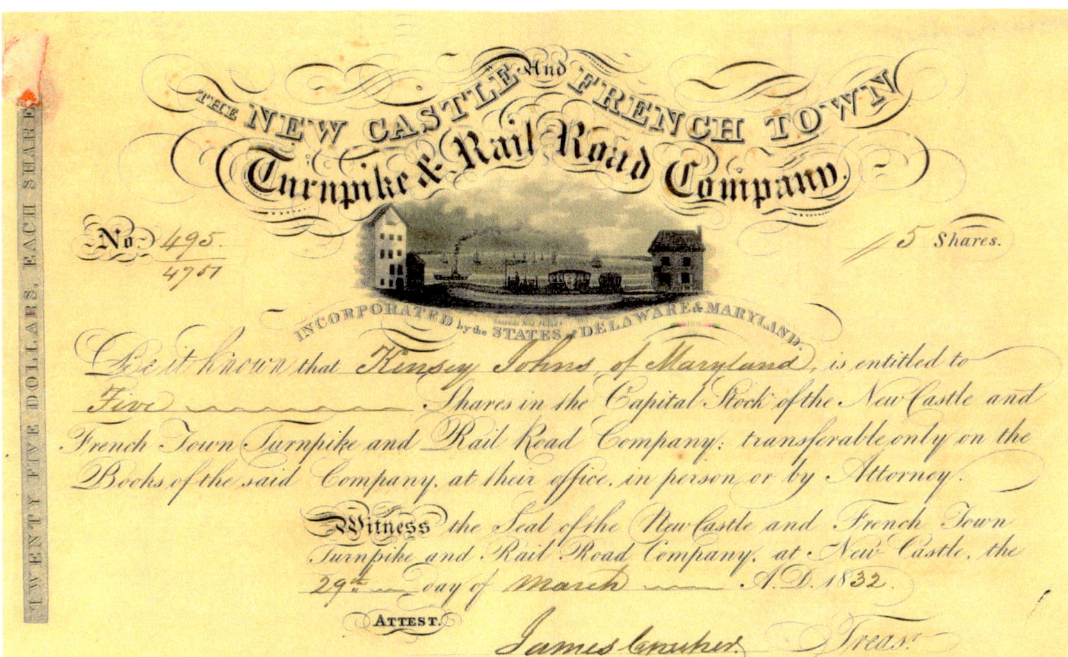

TWENTY FIVE DOLLARS, EACH SHARE

THE NEW CASTLE And FRENCH TOWN Turnpike & Rail Road Company.

No. 495. 4757

5 Shares.

INCORPORATED by the STATES of DELAWARE & MARYLAND.

Be it known that Kinsey Johns of Maryland, is entitled to Five Shares in the Capital Stock of the New Castle and French Town Turnpike and Rail Road Company; transferable only on the Books of the said Company, at their office, in person or by Attorney.

Witness the Seal of the New Castle and French Town Turnpike and Rail Road Company, at New Castle, the 29th day of March A.D. 1832.

ATTEST. James Crusher Treasr.

Stock sales were initially slow, probably due to the Maryland charter which allowed the Maryland portion of the company to be disbanded at any time the government so chose. This clause was due to the fear of governmental officials that the company would never be profitable. It was removed by the Maryland legislature in 1831. [*Courtesy of Keith Short & Jim Bowden*]

To say railroading was in its infancy would be an understatement. Due to this, many of the solutions to problems were all considered a first for railroading in the United States. The New Castle and Frenchtown was only the fourth railroad to be constructed in the country at the time. This culvert, located near the Elk River in Maryland, stands as a testament to those early engineers. [*Courtesy of the Delaware Public Archives*]

The rails nor the railroad bed were what are utilized today. In fact, railroad ties were not used at all. Stones, such as those shown here, were placed on the rail bed. The stones had holes drilled, wooden plugs placed and then a wooden rail, about six inches square and ten or twelve feet long was fastened to the stones by a piece of flat iron shaped like the letter "L". The stones were placed about three feet apart and each stone had two of these iron attachments, one on each side of the rail, spiked into the wooden plugs, Fifty-eight thousand stones were needed for the entire length of the railroad. Bars of thin flat iron imported from England were spiked on top of the wooden rails, with spikes manufactured by the Troy Nail Works of New York. It was learned quickly that these rails would spread apart, causing the train to derail. The solution was to place ties extending from one rail to the other to stop this from occurring. The practice continues to the modern era.

Its widely accepted that one of the first ticket booths for the New Castle & Frenchtown Rail Road stands today in old New Castle Delaware. It is near the exact location this railroad pioneer line began its near 17-mile trek to the Chesapeake Bay of Maryland. A new chapter of rail travel had come to America.

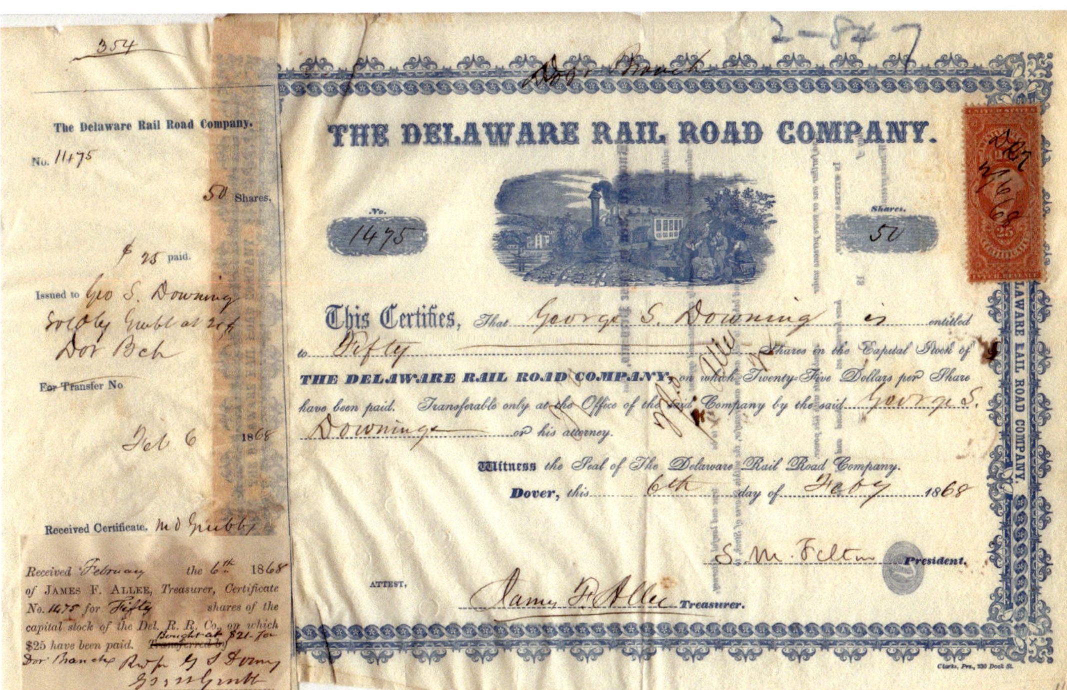

The Delaware Railroad was the first to build a rail line that ran the entire length of the state of Delaware. Connecting the New Castle and Frenchtown Rail Road and the four small railroads that had been reorganized in the 1830s to create the Philadelphia, Wilmington & Baltimore Railroad, the charter for the railroad had originally been approved on June 20th 1836. Sadly, it would take another twenty years to begin construction.

Judge Samuel Maxwell Harrington was the chief justice of the Delaware Supreme Court during the 1850s. He was also a champion of the railroad. Judge Harrington would travel the state in support of and lobbied heavily for the building of a rail line to southern Delaware. He realized that growth in the lower part of the state had become stagnant and locals needed a faster method to transport goods to the major cities of the Northeast.

Several towns in the state were created because of the railroad. Some were named after politicians such as the town of Clayton after Joshua Clayton, the first person to secure the Delaware Railroad charter and a U.S. Senator, as well as the small hamlet that sprung up about eight miles north of Harrington shown here. Felton was named after Samuel Felton, the president of the Philadelphia, Wilmington & Baltimore Railroad. [*Courtesy of the Felton Historical Society*]

PREVIOUS PAGE:

Below: The Delaware Railroad reached the small town of Clarks Corner in 1857. For a brief period, this town was the end of the line. The first passenger station was considered not much more than a barn. The station was rebuilt in the late 1860s and the town took on the name of its benefactor and became Harrington in honor of the man that had made the boom possible. The city continues to serve as a major hub of railroad activity for the area.

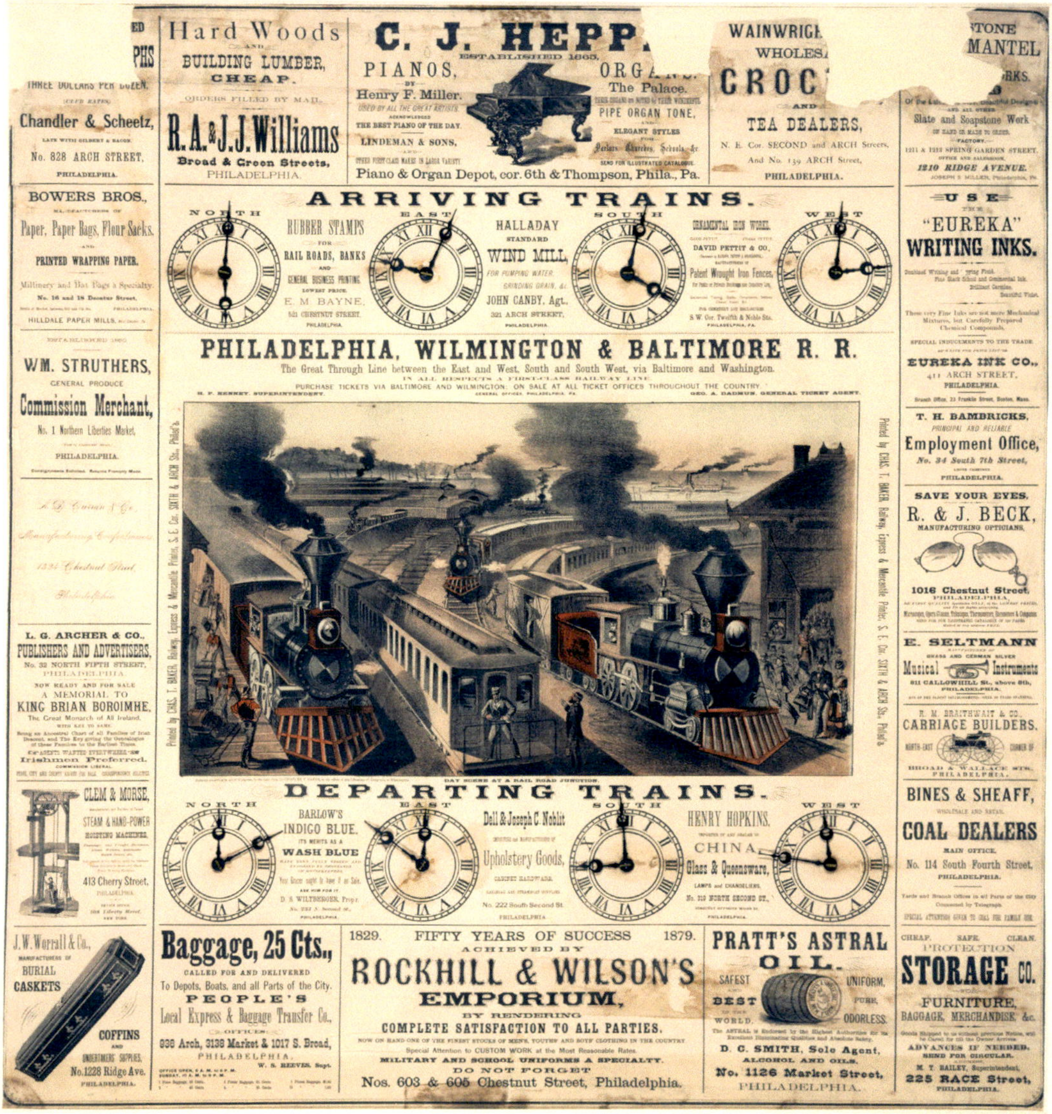

The Philadelphia, Wilmington & Baltimore Railroad was one of the first major railroad companies on the east coast of the United States. Founded in 1831, the company quickly established dominance in the region. Connecting the major cities of New York, Philadelphia and Baltimore, the railroad began to look to expand by becoming the major financial backer of smaller railroads over which it could dictate schedules and connect the famers directly to the major markets of the east coast.

The P. W. & B. played an unwitting role in the abolitionist movement in the United States by helping perhaps its most influential voice escape the bonds of slavery. Frederick Douglass, the famous abolitionist, was a slave in Baltimore when the chance to escape to freedom occurred. On September 3, 1838, with borrowed "seaman's protection," (a document obtained by his future wife, a free black woman, which was normally carried by free black sailors) Douglass used the vast knowledge of ships he had gained while working at the Fells Point Maryland shipping wharfs to talk his way to freedom while riding aboard a P. W & B. train bound for Philadelphia. This method of slavery escape became so frequent that a white person with knowledge of the black person had to sign for them to permit the person to board the trains by 1858.

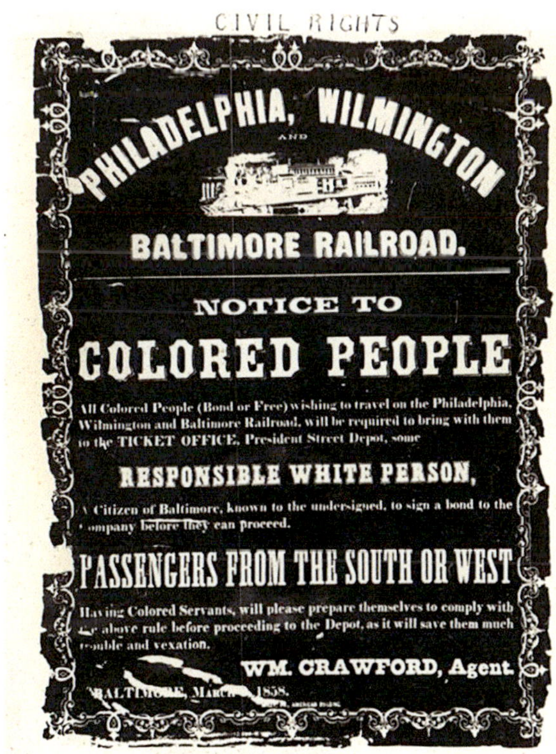

The P. W. & B. leased the Delaware Railroad in 1855, allowing for the two railroads to access each company's rails, opening up both freight and passenger services to most of the northern seaboard cities. The P. W. & B. constructed a new three-story Victorian-era station at Wilmington Delaware in 1907, replacing the smaller station built by the Delaware Railroad. The station still exists today and serves both Amtrak and Septa. [*Courtesy of the Delaware Public Archives*]

Delaware was the peach capital of the United States during the 1850s. As many as 800,000 trees were producing fruit at this time, and the railroad shipped them by the train full. Freight and passenger stops sprang up all along the line to serve the need to ship this and other goods. Woodside Delaware was founded in 1864 as a direct result of the need to ship agricultural goods via the railroad. [*Courtesy of the Delaware Public Archives*]

Middletown Delaware was already a busy city by the time the railroad came in the 1850s. Again another peach producer, the city grew along with the railroad. A steam engine rumbles through the town after picking up its passengers and cargo. Sadly, the entire peach crop was wiped out from a disease called the "Peach Yellows." Produce farmers turned to other crops such as apples and strawberries to make up for the loss, but the days of Delaware being the peach king were gone. [*Courtesy of Keith Short & Jim Bowden*]

By the 1880s, a bidding war had erupted over the P. W. & B. Both the Baltimore and Ohio and the Pennsylvania Railroad wanted to control the P. W. & B. A game of one-upmanship began between the two railroad giants with the PRR coming out the winner. The P. W. & B. continued to operate as its own entity despite the PRR board pulling the strings. A PRR steamer pulling a passenger train can be seen here speeding through the P. W. & B. yard in Wilmington, Delaware. [*Courtesy of the National Railroad Historical Society*]

With access to the PRR lines, a P. W. & B. engine can be seen here at the famous Broad Street Station in Philadelphia, Pennsylvania. A trip that took two days by horse and one day by steamboat now took hours by train. A businessman could board an early morning train, complete his business in the city, and be home to sleep in his own bed that same night. Seafood caught along the Delmarva Peninsula could be in the markets the next morning for consumers. [*Courtesy of the National Railroad Historical Society*]

The P. W. & B. either purchased or was a major financial backer of many of the short line railroads that would come to exist on the Delmarva Peninsula. Such was the case with the line than ran through Massey, Maryland. Built in 1867 by the Townsend Branch Railroad Company to connect the Delaware Railroad with the Queen Anne's and Kent Railroad, the line would fall under P. W. & B. control when it leased the Delaware Railroad.

Henry Wilhelm Photo/WestConn Chapter-NRHS collection 1929

Even as the Great Depression loomed, rail service was busier than ever. Seen here is a PRR Engine speeding past Ragan Tower near Newport, Delaware. The tower was originally constructed by the P. W. & B. and served until the 1970s. The signal bridge above pays homage back to the New Castle & Frenchtown Rail Road, as they created the signal system used by trains even today.

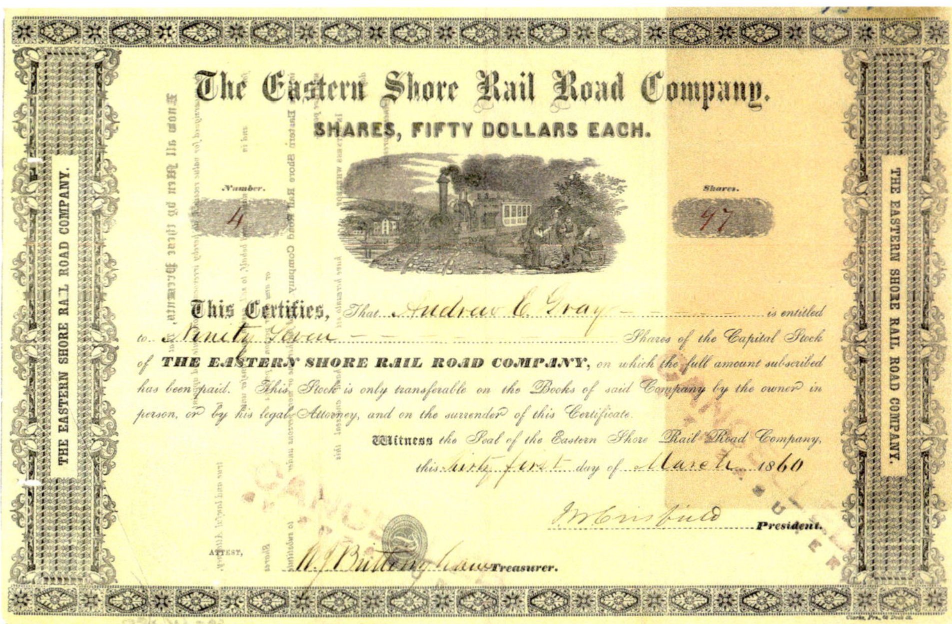

THE EASTERN SHORE RAIL ROAD COMPANY.

The Eastern Shore Rail Road Company.

SHARES, FIFTY DOLLARS EACH.

Number. 4

Shares. 97

This Certifies, That Andrew C. Gray is entitled to Ninety Seven Shares of the Capital Stock of THE EASTERN SHORE RAIL ROAD COMPANY, on which the full amount subscribed has been paid. This Stock is only transferable on the Books of said Company by the owner in person, or by his legal Attorney, and on the surrender of this Certificate.

Witness the Seal of the Eastern Shore Rail Road Company, this thirty first day of March 1860

J. W. Crisfield President.

Attest, W. J. Brittingham Treasurer.

THE EASTERN SHORE RAIL ROAD COMPANY.

The Eastern Shore Railroad was originally incorporated in 1833 and was planned to run the length of the peninsula but on the Maryland side. Imagine what might have changed if that had come to pass. In fact, the whole region could have even been in a different state. Maryland legislators failed by one vote to transfer the counties on the Eastern Shore of Maryland to Delaware during this time. [*Courtesy of Keith Short & Jim Bowden*]

Revitalized in 1853, the goal was to connect to the Delaware Railroad at the Maryland Delaware state line, with the first major stop being Salisbury, Maryland. The end of the line was at Crisfield, Maryland, one of the Eastern Shores jewels of seafood production. So rich in oysters, the first rail bed was on oyster shells. For a brief time, the line was managed by the P. W. & B. [*Courtesy of Keith Short & Jim Bowden*]

The Eastern Shore Railroad printed its own bank notes for a brief time. Notes such as this are very rare. Prior to the Civil War, there were over 8,000 different printed bank notes in the United States. These bill sometimes were accepted at face value and other times less, depending on the known financial stability of that business. The railroad would later move on to be a part of the first line to travel north and south through all three states.

THE JUNCTION & BREAKWATER R. R. CO.

No. 411 — 20 Shares

THE JUNCTION & BREAKWATER RAILROAD COMPANY.

This Certifies, That James S. Gibbons is entitled to Twenty Shares in the Capital Stock of

THE JUNCTION AND BREAKWATER RAIL ROAD COMPANY,

on which TWENTY-FIVE DOLLARS per Share have been paid, transferable only at the Office of the said Company, by the said James S. Gibbons or his Attorney.

Witness the Seal of THE JUNCTION & BREAKWATER RAIL ROAD COMPANY, at MILFORD, this Third day of April 1868

John W. Houston President.

ATTEST: Harbeson Hickman Treasurer.

As the railroad proved its value to communities, more and more towns clamored for service. This, along with the now proven method of delivery shown by the railroads before and during the Civil War, spurred what would become the greatest expansion of the rails across America our country would ever see. The Junction and Breakwater was one such railroad. Chartered in 1857, the railroad was to connect the Delaware Railroad to the ship port of Milford and continue to the shore.

The Junction and Breakwater began construction almost immediately, but then hit a snag just 4 miles east of where it began. Houston, Delaware, became the end of the line and the citizens of Milford, Delaware, constantly complained about the need to ride the muddy roads to reach the railroad station. Milford was a major shipping port and had lobbied very loudly to have the original railroad built there. Having lost that debate, they finally rejoiced when the train arrived on September 7, 1859.

One of the stops on this new line was Nassau, Delaware. An unincorporated area in the state, it was home to large orchards and other agricultural products. Nassau also enjoyed the distinction of being one of the four passenger stations along this new line. Part of the reason was nearby Belltown, Delaware, an African-American community. The line provided transportation for the community to areas allowing them to travel to work in the cities of Lewes and Rehoboth.

Initially the Junction and Breakwater stopped as its name implies, at the breakwater in Lewes, Delaware, reaching the pier in 1869 and officially opened on January 1, 1870. Several fishery canneries were built nearby and within a few years these businesses flourished and were shipping goods along the entire eastern seaboard. The trains literally went right out onto the water to load and offload goods.

The Junction and Breakwater was acquired on May 31, 1883 by the Delaware, Maryland and Virginia Railroad, which itself was acquired by the P. W. & B. in 1885, but continued to operate independently. Rehoboth Beach, Delaware, became the end of the line. This opened a new venture for passengers as the beginning of the twentieth century dawned: travel for leisure. Vacations, some for just the day, became a favorite pastime and the resort town boomed.

A second railroad was begun on March 31st, 1871, serving yet another area of Delmarva that was rich in agricultural goods that were in demand in the major cities of America. The Breakwater and Frankford connected small villages along its route and connected to the Junction and Breakwater at Georgetown, Delaware. Since railroads had to be incorporated in each state they traveled through, the line stopped at the Delaware-Maryland line. This line had originally been charted on February 2, 1835, as the Lewes & Millsboro Railroad.

Breakwater & Frankford and Worcester R. Rs.

RUNNING NORTH. / RUNNING SOUTH.

MAIL 1. A. M.	MIXED 2. A. M.	DISTANCES.	STATIONS.	MAIL 3. P. M.	PAS 4. P. M.	MIX. 4.
	5 00		LEAVE CHINCOTEAGUE, ARR.	7 00	†	‡
5 00	6 00		LEAVE FRANKLIN CITY, ARR.	6 15	8 00	2 00 P. M.
5 10	6 20	4"	STOCKTON,	5 55	7 50	1 40
5 20	6 40	7"	GIRDLETREE,	5 40	7 40	1 24
5 45	7 40	13"	SNOW HILL,	5 15	7 15	1 00
5 57	8 00	16"	WESLEY,	4 45	7 00	12 25
6 10	8 25	20"	QUEPONCO,	4 30	6.50	12 10
		"	*POPLAR,			
6 30	9 00	27"	BERLIN,	4 00	6 30	11 45
		29"	*FRIENDSHIP,			
6 45	9 25	32"	SHOWELLS,	3 40	6 15	11 25 A. M.
7 00	10 00	36"	SELBYVILLE,	3 25	6.00	11 10
7 12	10 20	40"	FRANKFORD,	3 00	5 40	10 48
7 18	10 40	42"	DAGSBOROUGH,	2 45	5 33	10 40
7 33	11 05	47"	MILSSBOROUGH,	2 20	5 18	10 20
		51"	*STOCKLEYS,			
8 10	12 10	56 AR	GEORGETOWN, LEAVE	1 45	4 50	9 45

‡Mixed train No. 4 connects with Steamer from New York at 9.45 a. m. on Tuesdays, Thursdays & Saturdays. †Passenger train No. 4 runs Mondays, Wednesdays & Fridays.

The Steamer Widgeon will leave Franklin City for Bloodgood's Wharf and Chincoteague Island, on Monday, Wednesday and Friday, at 6.30 a. m. Leave Chincoteague Island for Bloodgood's Wharf and Franklin City, at 4 p. m. Leave Franklin City for Wishart's Point, Monday, Wednesday and Friday, at 6 a. m. Returning, leave Wisharts Point for Franklin City, 12 m., stopping at Chincoteague and Bloodgood's Wharf, each way.

Local farmers brought their goods to be loaded on the train along this new line. Produce brokers would work with the local farmers, purchasing their crops and arranging payment to the farmers. Once the crop was ripe and picked, the farmers would deliver the goods to the freight stations nearest to them for shipping.

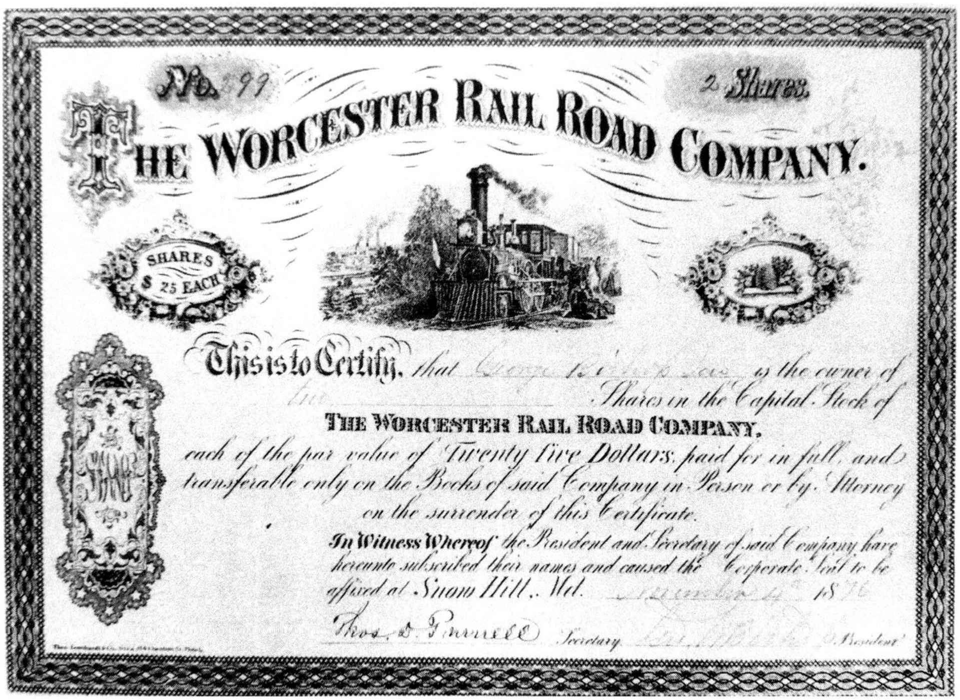

No. 99 2 Shares.

The Worcester Rail Road Company.

SHARES $ 25 EACH

This is to Certify, that [illegible] is the owner of [illegible] Shares in the Capital Stock of

THE WORCESTER RAIL ROAD COMPANY,

each of the par value of Twenty Five Dollars, paid for in full, and transferable only on the Books of said Company in Person or by Attorney on the surrender of this Certificate.

In Witness Whereof the President and Secretary of said Company have hereunto subscribed their names and caused the Corporate Seal to be affixed at Snow Hill, Md. [illegible] 187[illegible]

Thos. D. Purnell Secretary [illegible] President

The Worcester Railroad picked up where the other two railroads in the area left off, by building a railroad down the very eastern shore of Maryland to the very tip of Virginia, at a town called Franklin City. Their goods and passengers could travel by ferry to Chincoteague, Virginia. In 1883, these three railroads were incorporated in each of the states under one umbrella corporation named the Delaware, Maryland and Virginia. [*Courtesy of Keith Short & Jim Bowden*]

Chincoteague had been known since the first Native Americans came to the area for its abundant riches of seafood, particularly the millions of oysters that called its shallows home. With the railroad now, the seafood business exploded, sending canned oysters to the major cites by the boxcar full. Good and passengers were ferried across the sound on ships such as the *Chincoteague*. *[Courtesy of Keith Short & Jim Bowden]*

208 MARYLAND AND DELAWARE RAILROAD.

C. W. HUNTINGTON, President. | J. W. SCOTT, Auditor.
J. W. SCOTT, Sec'y and Treasurer. | J. L. CALDWELL, Superintendent.
General Offices—Easton, Md.

(*Philadelphia time.*)

Pass'ger.	Mls	*June 1, 1874.*	Mls	Pass'ger.
12 25 P.M.		lve... **New York**...arr.	199	5 10 P.M.
2 45 "		lve... **Baltimore**...arr.	151	1 15 P.M.
5 15 "		lve. **Philadelphia**.arr.	109	11 45 A.M.
6 35 "		lve.. **Wilmington**..arr.	81	10 15 "
8 25 "	0	lve.... **Clayton**[1]...arr.	44	8 20 "
8 40 "	5	.... Kenton.........	39	8 10 "
8 55 "	10	........Slaughter's.......	34	7 55 "
9 10 "	14	.........Marydell	30	7 45 "
9 20 "	17	.......Henderson........	27	7 35 "
9 30 "	20	.... Goldsboro........	24	7 25 "
9 45 "	24	.......Greensboro.......	20	7 10 "
[illegible] "	28	.........Ridgeley.........	16	6 55 "
10 10 "	32	.... .Hillsboro........	12	6 45 "
10 25 "	36	.........Cordova.........	8	6 30 "
10 35 "	41	........Woodland.......	3	6 20 "
10 50 P.M.	44	arr..... **Easton**....lve.	0	6 10 A.M.

CONNECTION.—[1]With Delaware Division Philadelphia, Wilmington & Baltimore R. R.

The Maryland and Delaware Railroad was begun in 1854 as one of the first rail lines to connect to the Delaware Railroad. The line's focus was again agriculture and seafood riches as it was to run from Smyrna Station (now Clayton) to Oxford Maryland. This 54-mile railroad short line would run through some of the area's richest farmlands and end at one of Maryland's oldest cities.

Greensboro Maryland was founded in the 1700s at the head of the Choptank River. As with so many of these small towns and hamlets, growth depended on moving goods to and from the area. And Greensboro was one of the lucky ones to receive the railroad to boost its economy. All the citizens of the area have turned out for an unknown special event.

Some stations just seemed to be placed in areas where the only town nearby was no more than a cluster of homes. Cordova, Maryland, would be a fine example of the railroad stopping in an area such as this. The town was founded as a Catholic missionary village and stayed a small agricultural area until the coming of the train. As with most locations that received a train stop, the area saw canneries and other factories grow around the railroad.

Right: As with so many of the early short line railroads, the Maryland and Delaware was sold and reorganized. In 1878, the railroad was sold and became the Delaware and Chesapeake Railroad. Eventually the line would, as almost all did, come under the control of the P. W. & B. The line continued to operate under its name until it was absorbed by the mighty PRR.

Below: One of the main stops on the Delaware and Chesapeake was Easton, Maryland. A small village prior to the railroad, the town was primed to grow, and grow it did. From only 1,400 citizens before the railroad, the town had nearly tripled in size by 1900. Three different railroads intersected in the city. Unique to this station is a water pipe from a water main to fill the engine, while most towns used above ground water tanks. [*Courtesy of Keith Short & Jim Bowden*]

PENNSYLVANIA

RAILROAD.

The Standard Railroad of America.

Philada, Wilm. & Balto. R. R.

DELAWARE AND CHESAPEAKE RAILWAY.

Schedule in effect July 7, 1900.
Passenger trains will run as follows:

North. Mail. A. M.	North. Pas. P. M.		South. Mail. A. M.	South. Pas. P. M.
7 00	1 56	Oxford,	11 28	7 41
7 07	2 03	Trappe,	11 21	7 48
7 20	2 16	Easton,	11 08	7 28
7 30	2 26	Chapel,	10 58	7 18
7 36	2 32	Cordova,	10 52	7 12
7 42	2 38	Queen Anne,	10 46	7 06
7 50	2 46	Ridgely,	10 38	6 58
8 00	2 56	Greensboro	10 28	6 48
8 09	3 05	Goldsboro,	10 19	6 39
8 15	3 11	Henderson,	10 13	6 33
8 21	3 17	Marydel,	10 07	6 27
8 28	3 24	Slaughter,	10 00	6 20
8 30	3 26	Hartley,	9 58	6 18
8 40	3 36	Kenton,	9 48	6 08
8 50	3 46	Clayton,	9 38	5 58
10 54	5 46	Philadelphia,	7 25	3 58
11 23	7 05	Baltimore.	6 25	3 20
A. M.	P. M.		A. M.	P. M.

Weather always played a role in the movement of the railroad. During the winter blizzards such as this one in 1899, travel was made difficult and sometimes impossible. Locomotives "The Talbot" and "The Easton" struggle to bring a train into the Easton, Maryland, station. Often gangs of workers would have to walk out to a train stranded in a snowstorm to dig out a snowbound train.

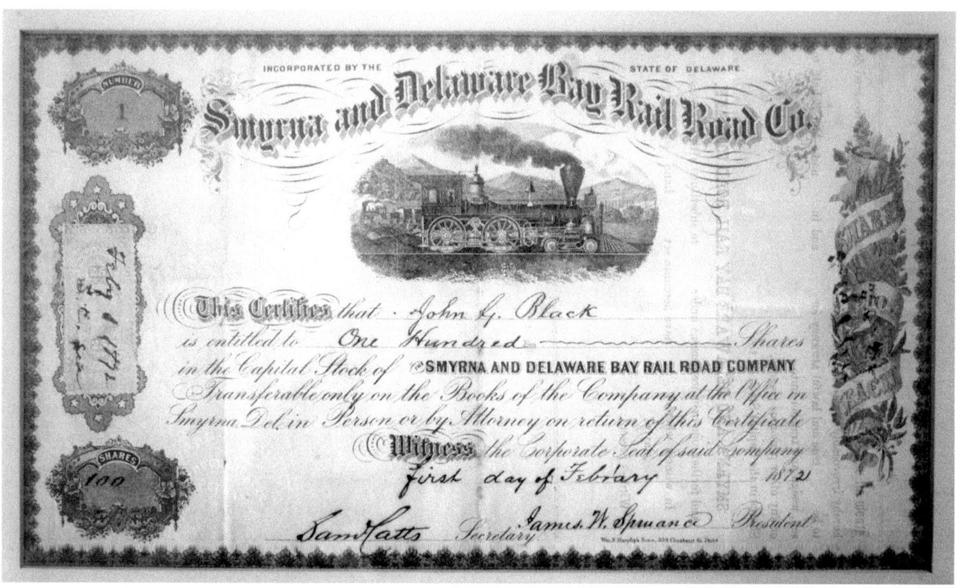

The Smyrna and Delaware Bay Railroad was the second segment of a rail line that stretched across the northern areas of Maryland and Delaware, connecting the upper Chesapeake Bay and Delaware River. Beginning in 1868, the railroad was first built in Kent County, Maryland. The line extended from the busy port city of Chestertown, Maryland, to Massey, Maryland. Then the portion in Delaware was built from Massey to Clayton, Delaware. This gave the line a connection to the Delaware Railroad. [*Courtesy of the Duck Creek Historical Society*]

Above: At the Delaware end of this line lay the resort town of Woodland Beach. One of the Mid-Atlantic's busiest and most popular seaside resort towns in the late 1800s, ferries traveled daily during the summer months from Pennsylvania, New Jersey, and New York. The train came directly to a wharf that allowed passengers and goods alike to be transferred directly onto the ships. [*Courtesy of the Delaware Public Archives*]

Right: While the line never really became the powerhouse railroad its owners dreamed of, its popularity with passengers grew with its connection to both bays and the ferries that took them to the major cities along the East Coast. Excursion trains and peach crops kept the small line busy during the warm months of the summer. [*Courtesy of the Sudlersville Community Betterment Club, Inc.*]

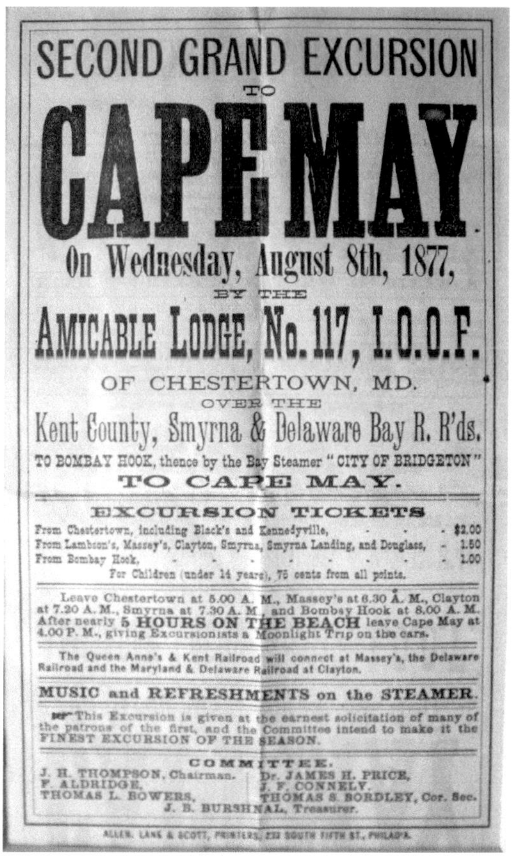

SECOND GRAND EXCURSION

TO

CAPE MAY

On Wednesday, August 8th, 1877,

BY THE

AMICABLE LODGE, No. 117, I.O.O.F.

OF CHESTERTOWN, MD.

OVER THE

Kent County, Smyrna & Delaware Bay R. R'ds.

TO BOMBAY HOOK, thence by the Bay Steamer "CITY OF BRIDGETON"

TO CAPE MAY.

EXCURSION TICKETS

From Chestertown, including Black's and Kennedyville, - - - $2.00
From Lambson's, Massey's, Clayton, Smyrna, Smyrna Landing, and Douglass, - 1.50
From Bombay Hook, - - - - - - - - 1.00
For Children (under 14 years), 75 cents from all points.

Leave Chestertown at 5.00 A. M., Massey's at 6.30 A. M., Clayton at 7.20 A. M., Smyrna at 7.30 A. M., and Bombay Hook at 8.00 A. M. After nearly 5 HOURS ON THE BEACH leave Cape May at 4.00 P. M., giving Excursionists a Moonlight Trip on the cars.

The Queen Anne's & Kent Railroad will connect at Massey's, the Delaware Railroad and the Maryland & Delaware Railroad at Clayton.

MUSIC and REFRESHMENTS on the STEAMER.

This Excursion is given at the earnest solicitation of many of the patrons of the first, and the Committee intend to make it the FINEST EXCURSION OF THE SEASON.

COMMITTEE.

J. H. THOMPSON, Chairman.
F. ALDRIDGE,
THOMAS L. BOWERS,
Dr. JAMES H. PRICE,
J. F. CONNELY,
THOMAS S. BORDLEY, Cor. Sec.
J. B. BURSHNAL, Treasurer.

ALLEN, LANE & SCOTT, PRINTERS, 233 SOUTH FIFTH ST., PHILAD'A.

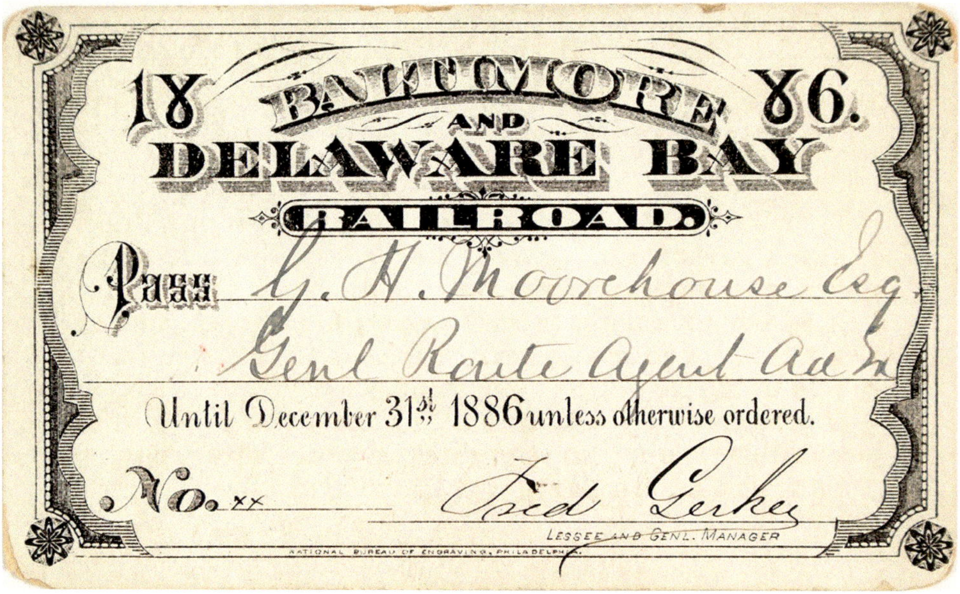

Interest in the line was sold to the New Jersey Southern Railroad in 1879 and reorganized under the name Baltimore and Delaware Bay Railroad. The main purpose was to divert the peach crop to New Jersey and beyond. The offices were even moved to New York City while the line was owned by New Jersey Southern. However, it was short lived, and in 1899 the line was again on its own. Finally, by 1902, the line had, as so many others, come under the P. W. & B. umbrella.

Commissioned in Maryland in 1866 and Delaware in 1867, the Dorchester and Delaware Railroad linked what as at the time the largest Maryland city on the Eastern Shore, Cambridge, with the Delaware Railroad at Seaford. Its first engine was named for its first President "W. Wilson Byrn." The engine was manufactured by the Baldwin Locomotive Company. *[Courtesy of the Dorchester County Historical Society]*

Built by the Jackson and Sharp Works in Wilmington, Delaware, this car was delivered to the company in 1874. While only 27 miles long, the railroad was always one of the more productive short lines ever built on Delmarva. The line was acquired by the P. W. & B. in 1883 and reorganized as the Cambridge and Seaford Railroad. [*Courtesy of the Delaware Public Archives*]

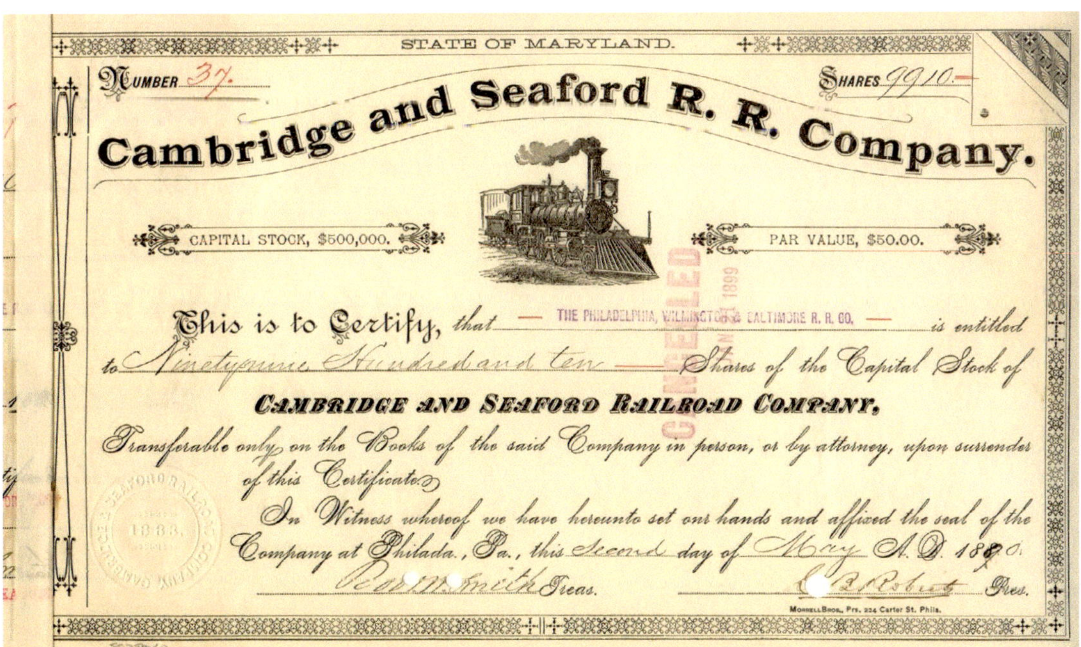
STATE OF MARYLAND.

NUMBER 37. SHARES 9910.

Cambridge and Seaford R. R. Company.

CAPITAL STOCK, $500,000. PAR VALUE, $50.00.

This is to Certify, that — THE PHILADELPHIA, WILMINGTON & BALTIMORE R. R. CO. — is entitled to Ninety-nine Hundred and ten Shares of the Capital Stock of

CAMBRIDGE AND SEAFORD RAILROAD COMPANY,

Transferable only on the Books of the said Company in person, or by attorney, upon surrender of this Certificate.

In Witness whereof we have hereunto set our hands and affixed the seal of the Company at Philada., Pa., this Second day of May A. D. 1890.

Treas. Pres.

CANCELLED

Following the reorganization, the Cambridge and Seaford Railroad continued to prosper. The rail line was one of the few that actually saw more gross revenues from freight than passengers, which was very rare for any railroad in the 1800s. The line became so valuable that property owners along the line saw the price per acre of their land quadruple in value.

Guy S. Burton of Cambridge, Maryland, was a trainman for the railroad during its busiest times. His uniform was typical of the day for anyone working on the passenger service lines. The conductor's job involved more than collecting tickets. He was the "captain" of the train. He supervised other train crew, looked out for the safety of everyone aboard, and made sure that every passenger paid the correct fare. *[Courtesy of the Dorchester County Historical Society]*

The Wilmington & Western Railroad was chartered in 1867, traveling from Wilmington, Delaware, to Landenberg, Pennsylvania. Originally called the Wilmington and Chester County Railroad, its name was changed a year later. With several mills existing along the Red Clay Creek, there was no shortage of business for the line. One of the six stations along the line was located in Marshallton, Delaware.

The lady standing on the B&O Railroad's Faulkland Station platform is Mary Agnes Mullins O'Rourke. Her father, John Mullins, came from Ireland in 1863. The station sat along the Red Clay Creek and while it never was a town, a large mill worked here for decades.

As with many short lines, the Wilmington and Western was short lived and sold at auction. The railroad was purchased for $5,000 in April 1877 and renamed the Delaware and Western. The new owners were able to make the new line much more profitable. But that was not the end of the story. Today the Wilmington & Western travels the rails again as a passenger excursion line, one of the most popular in the country.

When a resort opened along the railroad in the late 1880s at Brandywine Springs, the passenger business flourished as people from around the region came to the park to escape the summer heat. They came to enjoy the funhouse, pony rides, carousel, and live entertainment. The park closed in 1923. After this, passenger traffic fell dramatically on the line.

Another railroad giant had its eyes on this little railroad. The Baltimore and Ohio had lost the bidding war for the Philadelphia, Wilmington & Baltimore Railroad to the Pennsylvania Railroad. The B & O was desperate for its own rail line connecting Baltimore to the cities in the northeast. They had been paying access to the P. W. & B. and wanted to secure their own track. In 1883, the B & O was successful in purchasing the line. A new station was constructed in Wilmington, right next to the P. W. & B. station.

The Baltimore & Ohio famous Capital Limited service daily stopped in Wilmington, Delaware. The Capitol Limited was as an all-Pullman sleeping car train running from Pennsylvania Station in New York City to Chicago, via Washington, D.C. The B&O offered such luxuries in the 1920s as onboard secretaries, barbers, manicures, and valets. While having a few stations in Delaware, the B & O never saw prominence in the region.

Capital $400.000.

Shares $25.00 Each.

Wicomico and Pocomoke Rail Road Co.

No. 1

80 Shares.

WORCESTER COUNTY, MARYLAND

Incorporated 1864.

This Certifies that John B Myers is entitled to Eighty Shares in the Capital Stock of the Wicomico & Pocomoke Rail Road Co. Transferable only on the books of the Company in Person or by Attorney. Witness the Corporate Seal of said Company at Berlin, Md June 19th 1867

Secretary & Treasurer

President

Chartered originally in 1848, the Wicomico and Pocomoke Railroad was typical of the early railroad era, a train connecting two steamship landings, in this case, as the name says, the Wicomico and Pocomoke Rivers. The line, however, would not be built until after the Civil War and began service in 1868 with trains running from Salisbury to Berlin, Maryland. [*Courtesy of Keith Short & Jim Bowden*]

The first engine purchased by the company was from the Baldwin Locomotive factory and named the "L Showell" after Colonel Lemuel Showell, a large investor in the railroad. As was typical of the early wood burning steam engines, speed was not their forte. Frequently Colonel Showell would race his namesake engine on his horse and won the race to Berlin every time.

As with all these early lines, freight, particularly produce, was the name of the game. Loading produce onto the refrigerated cars in Berlin, Maryland, the Wicomico and Pocomoke freight business was very profitable. The watermelon crop for instance would see a profit of $9,000 in 1871, nearly a quarter-of-a-million dollars today. This was but one of several crops carried by the rail line.

In 1874, the line was expanded to the west side of the Sinepuxent Bay, just a ferry ride away from the resort town of Ocean City, Maryland. Two years later, a bridge was constructed over the bay and passengers and freight were delivered directly into the resort. But the desire for a true trans-peninsular line existed. So, in 1886, the Baltimore and Eastern Shore Railroad was created. [*Courtesy of Keith Short & Jim Bowden*]

The Baltimore and Eastern acquired the rights to the ferry terminal at Claiborne, Maryland, in 1890, thus ensuring that passengers and freight to and from the western shore of Maryland would be coming to their line. By achieving this goal, the line now ran from the Chesapeake Bay to the Atlantic Ocean, the first of its kind. Sadly, the line was barely completed when the railroad fell onto very hard economic times and was forced into bankruptcy and sold on August 29, 1894.

Every once in a while, beauty springs from the ashes and such was the case for the successor to the Baltimore and Eastern Shore Line. Christened the Baltimore, Chesapeake and Atlantic Railway, no sooner did the trains begin to run than the locals and travelers alike flocked to and became very romantic about this railroad. Maybe it was the logo, or maybe the fact it traveled to a beach resort at the time—but whatever the reason, its popularity was unmatched for its time.

The Baltimore, Maryland, steamer connection to the BC&A was obviously vital to the railroad's success. Multiple ships would travel the line, with even more help during the summer months. It would not be uncommon for double-header runs of up to seventeen cars per day to rumble into the beach resort. Special excursion trains would be run to meet other ferry lines just to use the BC&A route into Ocean City, Maryland.

Clairborne, Maryland, during the summer saw multiple passenger ferries a day, bringing families from the city to the Eastern Shore, connecting them to the railroads that would carry them on to their vacation destinations. Just as busy was the ferry line carrying freight business, crates filled with strawberries, peaches, and other goodies from the fields of Delmarva.

Shown here near St. Michaels, Maryland, the "Baltimore Flyer" as the train was known, was a special express train that ran during the summer months, and with only two stops along the way in Easton and Salisbury, Maryland, allowing vacationers to arrive in Ocean City in just over two hours, ready to begin their beach adventures. This line was so busy that during the World War I era, a non-stop train would run direct from ferry to sandy shores.

The BC&A, however, was not all about fun and sun. As with all railroads, freight was the main stay of the line. With thirty-two stops on its 108-mile journey, there were ample opportunities for local passenger and freight depots to off-load and on-load both revenue sources. Berlin, Maryland, had by this time been an established stop for other railroads and had a Union Station serving its citizens. The stop became a vital interchange for North–South freight and passengers. [*Courtesy of Keith Short & Jim Bowden*]

Not all the stations were as grand as Berlin, Easton, or Salisbury, Maryland. Mardela Springs, Maryland, is an example of the smaller passenger station freight depot combination buildings more commonly seen on Delmarva. This photo also best shows the BC&A nickname, "Black Cinder and Ashes," for the amount of smoke the engines bellowed forth.

There is no doubt that for the bulk of the passengers, Ocean City, Maryland, was their destination. The once small fishing village was now the premier summer resort destination for miles around. Prior to the railroad bridge being built, access was limited to the area by boat. Sadly, in 1933, a giant storm destroyed the railroad bridge to the area and it was never restored. Both the BC&A and the Maryland, Delaware and Virginia would go bankrupt. The MD&V was sold at foreclosure on May 7, 1923 and the BC&A was sold off in two parcels on March 29, 1928, and the Baltimore & Eastern took over the rail operations on November 28, 1928.

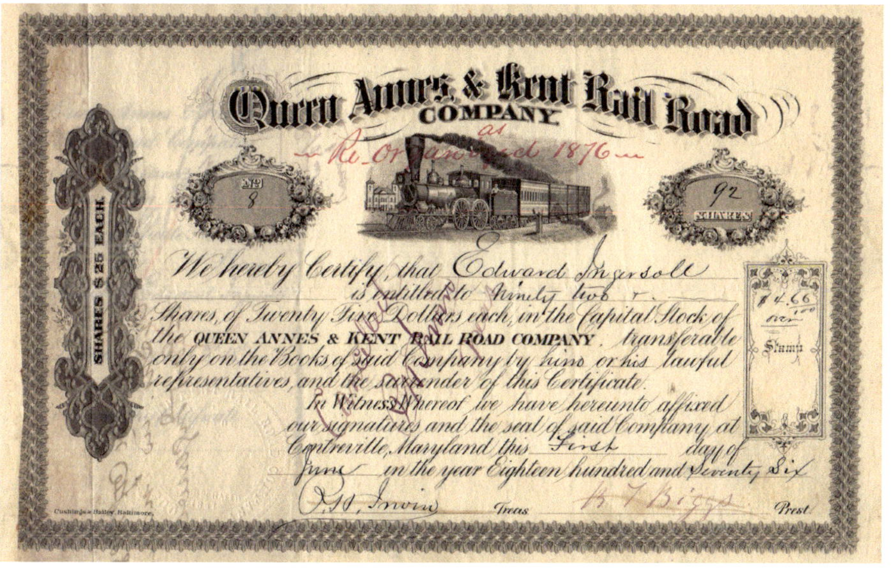

Queen Annes & Kent Rail Road COMPANY

Re-Organized at 1876

No 8

92 SHARES

SHARES $25 EACH.

We hereby Certify, that Edward Ingersoll is entitled to Ninety two Shares, of Twenty Five Dollars each, in the Capital Stock of the QUEEN ANNES & KENT RAIL ROAD COMPANY, transferable only on the Books of said Company by him or his lawful representatives, and the surrender of this Certificate.

In Witness Whereof we have hereunto affixed our signatures and the seal of said Company at Centreville, Maryland this First day of June in the year Eighteen hundred and Seventy Six

Treas. Prest.

Stamp

The ever-present battle over the riches of Delmarva's farm fields and waterways came up again in 1856. The Queen Anne's and Kent Railroad was proposed to connect the Chester River, which was getting its own railroad, to the upper portions of the Maryland and Delaware area, so Baltimore could pull more of these desired goods to the western shore instead of to the cities to the north. The railroad originally began in Massey, Maryland, with a connection to both the Kent County Railroad and later the Delaware Railroad at Townsend, Delaware.

Sudlersville, Maryland, was a simple stop along the rail line. The sleepy town was typical of the small towns along the railroad. The area, however, was rich in peach orchards and provided a large source of the fruit to send along to the major cities. The small town also had one large claim to fame, the birthplace of Baseball Hall of Famer, Jimmy Foxx. [*Courtesy of the Sudlersville Community Betterment Club, Inc.*]

The end of the line was Centerville, Maryland. A town of less than 900 people at the time the railroad was constructed, the town would come to see two separate train lines that would never meet. This was due to the failure of the Queen Anne's and Kent Railroad to reach its goal of the Chester River and on to Baltimore. With the failure of the railroad and its acquisition by the P. W. & B, more freight than ever headed north, which was in direct conflict with the entire reason for the rail lines construction. So when another Queen Railroad came to call on this small town, this time it would deliver on that promise. Despite being less than a mile apart, the two were so opposed to the major cities the other serviced, they would never connect. This is probably the best example of why so many early short line railroads failed in America. [*Courtesy of Keith Short & Jim Bowden*]

The next rail line on the peninsula saw consolidations, name changes, break ups, and more. The Delaware and Pennsylvania Railroad was the first to be incorporated in 1857. It then merged with the Doe Run and White Clay Creek Railroad, to become the Pennsylvania and Delaware Railroad in 1873. This line was split up again in 1879 into two lines, the Pomeroy and Newark Railroad and the Newark and Delaware City Railroad. Pomeroy, Pennsylvania, was the northern connection of the line. [*Courtesy of Ed Herbener Family*]

The end of the line was Delaware City, Delaware, a town with big dreams. Located at the eastern end of the Chesapeake and Delaware Canal, a major shipping lane, the area was also one of the best peach growing areas of the state. Locals hoped to create a major seaport with a railroad connection. While these dreams never panned out, today this section of the line serves large refineries in the area and is one of the few old lines still very active.

Above: The Wilmington and Northern Railroad began life as the Wilmington and Brandywine Railroad, but was reorganized in the 1870s. Heavily influenced by the DuPont family and factories of the area, the rail line ran from the Reading Railroad to the B & O in Wilmington, Delaware. The line also had six junctions with the PRR, so it was used for frequent freight and passenger interchanges.

The shops for the Wilmington and Northern were built in Wilmington, Delaware. And even after the line went bankrupt and was bought by the Reading Railroad, the shops continued to service engines for decades to come. As the photo shows, the yard was very active well into the 1940s.

PREVIOUS PAGE:

Below: A group of African Americans labor away on the railroad to construct the area near the DuPont Gun Powder works. This area was so populated by people working for the DuPont Company that eventually a community with its own trolley line was setup to move workers to and from their homes directly to the factory sites on the Brandywine River.

The Queen Anne's Railroad was the last of the major rail construction projects undertaking on the Delmarva Peninsula. Begun in 1894, the ambitious project was to create a connection from Baltimore by ferry to Kent Island, Maryland, then travel by rail to the Delaware Seashore, where it would connect again to a ferry ride across the bay to Cape May, New Jersey. [*Courtesy of the Kent Island Heritage Society*]

The "Queen Anne" side-wheeler was built in 1899 specifically for the company's Queenstown dock by the Baltimore Dr Dock Company at a cost of $75,000. In 1902, a sister ship named the *Queen Caroline* was built and placed into the Lewes, Delaware, to Cape May, New Jersey, portion of the service. This ferry halted when the company went under, but in the 1950s was reborn, and service continues today as the Cape May & Lewes Ferry. [*Courtesy of the Kent Island Heritage Society*]

Built for the Queen Anne's Railroad in 1901 by the Jackson and Sharp Company of Wilmington, Delaware, the beautiful coach car was very detailed and high-end for its day. The scrollwork on the end of the car at the canopy area and the striping of even the trucks shows the true Victorian style of the era. There is no doubt that this coach was the pride of the line. [*Courtesy of the Delaware Public Archives*]

One of the stops on the line was Milton, Delaware. Long a shipping port and mill area, the town already had a sizable population before the coming of the Queen Anne's Railroad. Several local men and young boys pose in 1904 while awaiting the arrival of the train.

Despite the connections from shore to shore, the line remained a financial albatross. On January 28 1905, the line fell into the hands of the railroad that had only ten years before fought against it ever being built, the PRR. The fight was so fierce that when the Queen Anne's Railroad crossed at grade with the Delaware Railroad (controlled by the PRR) at Greenwood, Delaware, the PRR made them build a separate passenger and freight station a block north of their station, thereby not allowing a union station to exist, just to cause an inconvenience to travelers. The new line was christened the Maryland, Delaware and Virginia Railroad. The line was placed under the control of the Baltimore, Chesapeake and Atlantic Railroad and as such, several similarities, right down to the font used on paper goods, was shared between the two.

Love Point, Maryland, now served as the ferry dock for both passenger and freight service. The docks were moved here to shorten the ferry trip and thus save time. The "Westmorland" replaced the "Love Point" in 1909 after the ferry was destroyed by fire. The M. D. & V and the BC&A together in 1907 showed just how large their water operation was. Thirty-six boats, traversing points along the Chesapeake Seaboard, carried over 500,000 tons of freight with a value of over 33 million dollars, and nearly 900,000 passengers. [*Courtesy of the Kent Island Heritage Society*]

With the Maryland, Delaware and Virginia also being a tourist line, Victorian-era men and women used the ferries and rails to travel the countryside. With service to Lewes and Rehoboth, Delaware, several of Baltimore's finest could be seen on the lines. Here in 1909, Mrs. Emma Sadler can be seen riding the coach car from Love Point. The train would arrive in Rehoboth each night bringing the newest movie for the theater. The reels would be run down from the station just in time for the 9 p.m. show. [*Courtesy of the Kent Island Heritage Society*]

Kent Island, or the Kent Narrows as the waterway was known, was one of the many stops along the railway. This village was the first permanent English settlement in Maryland, going back to 1631, and the third oldest in the country. The crab, fishing and oyster harvests made this village one of the major seafood shipping stops on the line. The beautiful wooden trestle bridge can be seen in this 1922 photograph. [*Courtesy of the Kent Island Heritage Society*]

Denton, Maryland, was another stop on the line that had its own unique story. Near the station was a very popular ice cream shop. As the train was on its way from the beach area, an order would be taken from the passengers, sent ahead, and the shop would have the proper cones ready when the train arrived. This ice cream was a great summer treat, as this store was in business long after the trains stopped, because this author has had his fair share from there, too.

Corrected to June 28th, 1930—
(except as noted)

Note Carefully, Effective dates shown herein.

The Baltimore and Virginia Steamboat Company

Baltimore and Eastern Railroad Company

Rail and Steamer Lines

Time Table

THE TIME SHOWN IN THIS TABLE IS

EASTERN STANDARD TIME

R. K. ROCHESTER, General Manager

R. H. SOULSBY, Gen. Pass. Agent

No. 116

DESTROY ALL OTHER ISSUES

10,000-6-30

Sadly both sister railroads went under in 1928 and were sold off, with most of the line being abandoned. The line that took over parts of the MD&V and all of the BC&A was renamed the Baltimore and Eastern Railroad, which had begun it original operations in 1923. The line then shifted all ferry operations to Love Point, and the line ended in Ocean City, Maryland, combining both lines. The line to Rehoboth, Delaware, was sold off to another railroad.

The Baltimore and Eastern operated parts of the line for decades, but the PRR was behind the scenes, slowly abandoning lines, whether due to a lack of freight or other reasons, such as the violent storm in August 1933 that destroyed the bridge to Ocean City, Maryland. For decades later, Baltimore and Eastern painted cars could be seen working on the PRR lines.

As the breakup and abandonments began in the smaller areas of the peninsula, some areas still seemed viable for service. Enter the Maryland & Delaware Coast Railroad in 1927. A group of investors purchased to line from Denton, Maryland, to Lewes, Delaware, then added a bus service to Rehoboth, Delaware, so passenger service could continue as well. Here is the "302 Lewes," the company's four-wheel drive, gasoline-powered unit produced by J. G. Brill Company.

Maryland & Delaware Seacoast Railroad took over this operation in 1932, following the bankruptcy of its namesake. This company fared no better and by 1934, this company failed as well. The line then fell back into the Baltimore and Eastern Railroad and another portion became the property of the Delaware, Maryland and Virginia. Today, a large portion of this entire line has become a part of the Rails to Trails bike program.

Coal was king and the railroads moved it. From the earliest days of coal mining, small ore cars to traction lines, coal moved by the rails. With the coming of the coal fired steam engine, the demand for the black rock skyrocketed. Mines were in the north, but the south needed this valuable resource. Cheaper and faster ways required innovation. Into this stepped William Lawrence Scott, a coal mine owner and member of the Unites States House of Representatives. Scott wanted a quicker and cheaper way to get his coal to the city of Norfolk, Virginia, and beyond. Currently the valuable resource had to travel around the Chesapeake Bay, taking time and costing him money. The question was how? He pitched his rail idea to the Pennsylvania Railroad with no luck, except for one man who shared Scott's vision.

Alexander Johnston Cassatt was a man of extraordinary vision that combined business savvy with an engineer's mind. The result was someone who was a vice president with the Pennsylvania Railroad by age thirty-seven and oversaw the construction of massive projects such as the railroad tunnels under the Hudson and East Rivers in New York City. When he later became president of the PRR, he managed to double the company's assets during his tenor. Cassatt saw that Scott was onto a brilliant idea, so he resigned from PRR and jumped headfirst into the project. Cassatt personally scouted out the route for the line and helped get the financial backing needed to complete the project.

Cassatt also used already existing railroads to help with the project. The Worcester & Somerest Railroad was the first of these dominos. The line was broken into the Peninsula Railroad Company of Maryland and the Peninsula Railroad Company of Virginia. The Eastern Shore Railroad was also brought under the corporate umbrella, and finally, on September 19, 1882, the New York, Philadelphia and Norfolk Railroad Company was formed. For decades, the line was referred to as the "Cassatt Line South."

Now the N. Y. P. & N. was official and track work began almost immediately. Using the Eastern Shore and Peninsula Railroads as a starters, the construction began in April of 1884. Progress was swift from the point south of Pocomoke City, Maryland, to the water's edge. The last spike was driven six months later on October 25, 1884. There was no town at the end of the line, no houses, and no roads, but nonetheless the N. Y. P. & N. had arrived at its destination and the lights of Norfolk and the ultimate goal could be seen, a mere thirty-six miles away. [*Courtesy of the Cape Charles Historical Society*]

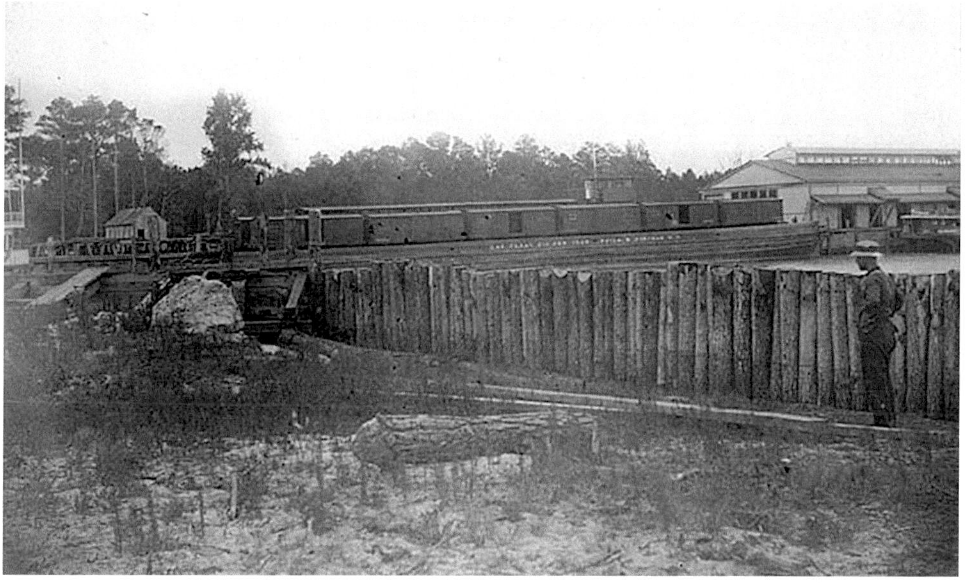

No railroad in history had ever attempted what Cassatt was planning next. Barges, designed to carry eighteen cars at a time, pulled by tugs powerful enough to haul the massive weight in tidal waters, were designed. Pennsylvania Railroad was given one last chance to build the line, but again declined, so Scott and Cassatt pledged their own fortunes to each other and the project and moved ever forward. [*Courtesy of the Cape Charles Historical Society*]

Scott, while no engineer, was a businessman at heart. He knew he needed a town because he needed manpower. So, the surrounding area was purchased, and the city laid out in a grid. Streets were laid out, with the North and South street being named after fruits, while the East and West streets were named after Virginia's Governors. The new city was christened Cape Charles City. A few men, believing in the dream, jumped into the fray. A hotel was proposed, and many believed the town would have over 5,000 inhabitants in just a few short years. [*Courtesy of the Cape Charles Historical Society*]

Only one challenge remained. At the time the line was completed to the proposed dock area, the waterway could not support the proposed tugs or barges. In fact, during dry spells it could barely float a child's toy. But again, Cassatt, ever the engineer and man he was, stood ready to tackle the problem. Unable to gather financial backing for the dredging, Cassatt funded this part of the project, again using his own fortunes. While on the opposite shore, work was underway to build the facilities needed to interchange the cars with the railroads located on the Elizabeth River. [*Courtesy of the Cape Charles Historical Society*]

On November 17, 1884, in less than a year, passenger service began from Cape Charles, Virginia, to Norfolk, Virginia. The side-wheeler, "Jane Mosley," had the honor of making this inaugural run. While passenger service started light, and freight service was limited to just what the ferry could hand load, the project was off, and with it, Scott and Cassatt's personal fortunes. [*Courtesy of the Cape Charles Historical Society*]

What both men desperately desired was for the freight service they had both envisioned to become a reality. And on March 12, 1885, the tug "Norfolk," pulling car float No. 1, streamed into Norfolk, Virginia, with a load of twelve freight cars. No doubt both men held their breath as this first crossing occurred. Much to their relief, the entire project was a huge success. Traffic, both passenger and freight, quickly began to boom. [*Courtesy of the Cape Charles Historical Society*]

In 1886, the first train crew from Delmar, Maryland, pulled into Cape Charles, Virginia, fulfilling the dream that so many had fought for and invested in. All knew the train would open their rural area to the rest of America. Within months, both passenger and freight business was booming. Larger ferries and car floats had to be ordered to keep up with the volume the N.Y. P. & N experienced. [*Courtesy of the Cape Charles Historical Society*]

Workers that brought that first train to town: first row (seated, left to right) George Barr, engineer, Joe Restin, Brakeman; second row (standing, left to right) Dan Parker, fireman, Elijah John Melson, luggage master, William C. "Bill" Truitt, conductor. [*Courtesy of the Cape Charles Historical Society*]

Two unknown men pose near the newly completed train station at Cape Charles. In just a few years, this terminal would be replaced by an even larger structure due to the number of passengers using the line. Rails pulled directly up to the right side of the station, while the passenger ferries pulled up on the left, allowing passengers to directly transfer from one mode of transportation to the other. [*Courtesy of the Cape Charles Historical Society*]

Directly located next to the passenger station and steamship docks, the freight docks were just as busy. The early ferries could carry on twelve freight cars; however, within a few years, larger barges and tugs upped that number to eighteen cars. In the foreground, another ferry loading dock is being built. [*Courtesy of the Cape Charles Historical Society*]

By the early 1900s, the sheer number of freight cars required three loading docks. Heavier steel freight cars became the normal, as well as refrigerated cars, requiring the N.Y. P. & N. to construct barges that could hold the excess weight, and tugs that could pull these massive loads across the bay. [*Courtesy of the Cape Charles Historical Society*]

By 1890, you can see the freight loading docks have been moved to accommodate the busier port area. Two full barges are under steam, a passenger ferry is sitting at the terminal dock, a coal car is sitting on the coal loading area, and a passenger train is at the terminal. This sight would occur multiple times a day as the port became a beehive of activity. [*Courtesy of the Cape Charles Historical Society*]

103

NEW YORK, PHILADELPHIA and NORFOLK R.R.

NEW SHORT ROUTE

Running Through Cars, without change, from NEW YORK to the Eastern Shore of the Chesapeake,

Old Point Comfort and Norfolk, Va.,

And connecting at NORFOLK, VA., and PORTSMOUTH, VA., with trains for CHARLESTON, SAVANNAH, FLORIDA and ALL POINTS IN THE SOUTH.

Through Pullman Sleeping Cars between New York and Cape Charles, and Philadelphia and Cape Charles on Trains 97 and 82.

Through Buffet Parlor Cars between Philadelphia and Cape Charles on Trains 94 and 45.

THROUGH TIME-TABLE.

Acc. 127	Acc. 91 NO'N	Acc. 3	Old Point Express. No. 45	Mail. No. 85	Norfolk Express. No. 97	Mls	*December 1, 1898.*	Phila. Accom. No. 92	N. York Express. No. 94	Norf. & N.Y. Exs No. 82	Acc. 62 P.M.	Acc 116
	12 50		7 50 A.M.		7 40 P.M.		lv New York West 23d St. ar	3 15 P.M.	8 45 P.M.	8 05 A.M.	10 20	
	1 00		8 00 A.M.		8 00 P.M.		lv New York Cort. or Des. Sts. ar	3 03 P.M.	8 38 P.M.	7 43 A.M.	10 08	
	P.M.						LEAVE] [ARRIVE				P.M.	
	1 26		8 25 A.M.		8 32 P.M.		Newark, N. J.	2 35 P.M.	7 54 P.M.	7 18 A.M.	9 40	
	P.M.						LEAVE] [ARRIVE				P.M.	
	3 46		10 20 A.M.	†7 25 A.M.	11 10 P.M.		Philadelphia	12 06 NO'N	5 43 P.M.	5 10 A.M.	7 38	
	P.M.						LEAVE] [ARRIVE				P.M.	
	4 27		11 04 A.M.	8 13 A.M.	11 56 P.M.		Wilmington	11 19 A.M.	4 59 P.M.	4 15 A.M.	6 50	
	P.M.						LEAVE] [ARRIVE				P.M.	
	5 00		8 23 A.M.	6 25 A.M.	7 53 P.M.		Baltimore	12 35 NO'N	6 55 P.M.	6 19 A.M.	8 40	
	†7 34		†1 51 P.M.	†11 37 A.M.	*2 55 A.M.	0	lve. Delmar arr.	7 55 A.M.	2 09 P.M.	1 00 A.M.	3 25	
	7 44		2 02 »	11 50 A.M.	3 06 »	6	Salisbury	7 35 »	1 56 »	12 47 N'HT	3 10	
	7 56		--	12 01 NO'N	--	10	Fruitland	7 18 »	--	--	2 57	
	8 01		--	12 06 »	--	13	Eden	7 08 »	--	--	2 51	
	8 06	A.M.	--	12 11 »	--	15	Loretto	7 02 »	--	--	2 46	
	8 14	†6 35	2 24 »	12 20 »	3 29 »	19	Princess Anne	6 56 »	1 31 »	12 20 »	2 40	
A.M.	8 20	6 49	2 33 P.M.	12 30 NO'N	3 33 A.M.	22	arr. King's Creek lve.	6 40 A.M.	1 25 P.M.	*12 10 N'HT	2 35	A.M.
†11 00		6 40	2 33 P.M.			22	lve. King's Creek arr.	6 25 A.M.	1 35 P.M.			9 15
11 15		6 45	2 55 »			24	Westover	6 13 »	1 10 »			8 55
11 25		6 51	3 10 »			28	Kingston	5 58 »	1 00 P.M.			8 30
11 40		6 57	3 30 »			32	Marion	5 49 »	12 46 NO'N			8 10
11 50		7 03	3 40 »			34	Hopewell	5 38 »	12 37 »			7 55
12 05		7 15	4 00 P.M.			38	arr. Crisfield lve.	†5 30 A.M.	†12 30 NO'N			†7 45
NO'N	8 20	A.M.	2 33 P.M.	12 30 NO'N	3 33 A.M.		lve. King's Creek arr.	6 40 A.M.	1 25 P.M.	12 10 N'HT	2 33	A.M.
	8 40		2 46 »	1 00 P.M.	3 49 »	31	Pocomoke	†6 10 A.M.	1 06 P.M.	11 55 P.M.	†12 10	
	P.M.		2 57 »		4 01 »	37	New Church		12 53 NO'N	11 43 »	P.M.	
			3 10 »		4 14 »	45	Hallwood		12 37 »	11 32 »		
			3 24 »		4 26 »	52	Parksley		12 22 »	11 18 »		
			3 37 »		4 38 »	58	Tasley		12 11 NO'N	11 05 »		
			3 52 »		4 52 »	65	Keller		11 52 A.M	10 46 »		
			4 04 »		5 05 »	[illegible]	Exmore		11 40 »	10 31 »		
			4 17 »		5 19 »	79	Bird's Nest		11 26 »	10 16 »		
			4 31 »		5 33 »	86	Eastville		11 14 »	10 01 »		
			4 50 »		5 55 »	95	arr. Cape Charles lve.		10 55 »	9 40 »		
			6 50 »		8 00 »	119	arr. Old Point Comfort lve.		8 40 »	7 10 »		—
			7 50 »		9 00 »		Norfolk		7 45 »	6 00 »		
			8 00 P.M.		9 10 A.M.	131	Portsmouth		†7 30 A.M.	*5 30 P.M.		
							ARRIVE] [LEAVE					

Leave New York from West Twenty-third, Cortlandt or Desbrosses Street Stations of the Pennsylvania R.R.

All Through Tickets of foreign lines issue convey a stop over privilege at Old Point Comfort only.

FIVE HOURS SHORTER THAN BY ANY OTHER LINE.

Time from 1 00 p.m. to 12 59 night is printed in dark type. Connecting points in bold-faced type. See Index of Stations.

By 1898, the New York, Philadelphia & Norfolk was one of the busier railroads on the eastern seaboard. With now over twenty stops on the line, passenger and freight business continued to soar. Farmers would wait for hours just to load their produce onto the cars at each stop.

The Cassatt Tower was named for the genius that made the railroad possible. In fact, Cassatt had personally designed the swing bridge over the Pocomoke River where the tower was located. His personal dream cut what was a two-day trip from New York City to Norfolk down to just under twelve hours.

Pocomoke, Maryland, was the head of the line. While the New York, Philadelphia and Norfolk had acquired the right to travel rails down to this point, it was from here the N.Y. P. & N. began their own rails. The station was one of their first built, and as with several of their stations, this was a two-story structure. The second story was at first the home for the station masters since so many of these stations were not initially near a town.

TO DELMAR
EXMORE

Coal ran both the trains and the all of the shipping vessels for the line. In order to load the coal easily and quickly onto the ferries and tugs, a ramp was constructed alongside the dock area where coal ore cars could be parked over a chute. Then the coal could be directed into the holds of the vessel's coal storage area. [*Courtesy of the Eastern Shore Railway Museum*]

PREVIOUS PAGE:

Above: Exmore, Virginia, is the perfect example of the railroad making a town. Exmore's beginning is probably best described by H. C. Davis of Willis Wharf, who went to Exmore as a railroad employee shortly prior to the railroad's passing through the soon-to-be town: "It wasn't known as anything—there was nothing there." This was because the towns of this area were all located on the water, because of the shipping and seafood industries. [*Courtesy of the Eastern Shore Railway Museum*]

Below: Engine No. 10 was produced for the railroad by the Baldwin Locomotive Factory, located in Philadelphia, Pennsylvania. Built in 1902, the new locomotive is shown here with supervisor Jesse Oren (in vest and derby hat) and his crew. The yard crews were always very proud of their equipment, especially the engines, as they were the identity of the company. [*Courtesy of the Eastern Shore Railway Museum*]

NEW YORK, PHILADELPHIA & NORFOLK RAILROAD.

"CAPE CHARLES ROUTE." Adams Express Co.

WM. A. PATTON, President,
A. J. COUNTY, Vice-President,
O. J. De ROUSSE, Secretary,
J. F. FAHNESTOCK, Treasurer,
SAMUEL PORCHER, Purchasing Agt, } Broad Street Station, Philadelphia, Pa.
H. C. CARLILE, Auditor, Philadelphia, Pa.
WM. L. MARKLEY, Assistant Auditor, "
R. B. COOKE, Traffic Manager, Norfolk, Va.
C. I. LEIPER, Superintendent, Cape Charles, Va.
General Offices—Philadelphia, Pa.

45	47	43	81	49	Miles	*June 27, 1914.*	82	48	46	80	50	1048
Noon	A M	.....	.....	P M	.....	lve.. **New York**.arr.	P M	P M	P M	.....	A M	P M
12 08	8 00	.....	.....	9 00	.....	...*Penna. Station*...	7 23	8 00	11 18	.....	7 32	9 18
12 00	8 00	A M	.....	9 00	0	...*Hudson Term*...	7 26	8 00	11 20	.....	7 34	9 20
3 00	10 00	†7 25	.....	11 17	90.0	..Phila. (*Broad St.*)..	5 03	5 48	8 35	.....	5 00	6 29
3 44	10 44	8 19	.....	12 01	116.7	....**Wilmington**....	3 49	4 55	7 50	.....	4 05	5 40
6 58	1 27	11 38	.....	3 00	214.3	arr... **Delmar**.. lve.	12 07	2 20	4 15	.....	12 48	2 58
P M	P M	A M	A M	A M	.....	LEAVE] [ARRIVE	A M	P M	P M	P M	Night	P M
†7 12	*1 35	†11 50	†6 50	*3 09	0	....**Delmar**[1].... ♁	11 30	2 10	4 05	10 30	12 38	2 49
7 26	1 48	12 05	7 03	3 20	5.9	...**Salisbury**[2]... ♁	11 18	2 00	3 50	10 15	12 23	2 35
7 35	*e*1 56	12 20	7 12	– –	9.7	......Fruitland.... ♁	11 07	*c*1 48	3 26	9 55	– –	*c*2 15
7 41	– –	12 26	7 18	– –	12.9	.... Eden ..... ♁	11 00	– –	3 16	9 49	– –	– –
7 46	*e*2 04	12 31	7 23	– –	15.6	.......Loretto.......	10 54	*c*1 41	3 10	9 43	– –	*c*2 04
7 53	2 11	12 40	7 30	3 38	19.1	.**Princess Anne**. ♁	10 47	1 35	3 00	9 35	11 56	1 57
8 07	•2 17	12 50	7 36	– –	21.6	...**King's Creek**. ♁	10 41	1 29	2 41	9 25	– –	– –
8 26	2 33	1 14	7 52	3 55	30.9	....**Pocomoke**.. ♁	10 25	1 09	2 25	9 10	11 36	1 35
8 40	*h*2 41	1 26	8 04	*a*4 06	37.3	....New Church.. ♁	10 12	*t*12 58	2 08	8 55	*b*11 24	1 23
8 49	– –	1 36	8 13	– –	41.4	......Oak Hall.... ♁	10 04	– –	1 57	8 45	*r*11 15	– –
8 54	*d*2 49	1 41	8 18	*a*4 18	42.7	...Makemie Park. ♁	10 01	*t*12 49	1 52	8 39	*b*11 11	1 12
9 00	*h*2 53	1 47	8 24	*a*4 25	45.0	......Hallwood.... ♁	9 56	*t*12 44	1 46	8 32	*b*11 05	1 06
9 09	*d*2 59	1 58	8 34	*a*4 32	48.8	......Bloxom...... ♁	9 46	*t*12 39	1 36	8 21	*b*10 56	12 59
9 20	*h*3 04	2 10	8 45	*a*4 39	52.4	......Parksley.... ♁	9 37	*t*12 34	1 26	8 12	*b*10 50	12 53
9 31	3 13	2 21	8 57	*l*4 49	58.0	.......Tasley...... ♁	9 25	12 25	1 13	8 00	10 39	12 43
9 36	*d*3 17	2 26	9 02	*a*4 54	59.7	.......Onley.... ♁	9 20	*t*12 21	1 06	7 56	*b*10 36	12 38
9 42	*d*3 22	2 31	9 08	*a*5 00	62.7	.......Melfa...... ♁	9 14	*t*12 17	1 00	7 50	*b*10 31	12 32
9 47	*h*3 27	2 37	9 13	*a*5 05	65.2	.......Keller ..... ♁	9 08	*t*12 13	12 53	7 43	*b*10 26	12 26
9 52	*d*3 32	2 43	9 18	*a*5 12	67.7	.......Painter .... ♁	9 02	*t*12 09	12 47	7 35	*b*10 19	12 20
9 56	– –	2 48	9 22	– –	70.6	....Belle Haven.. ♁	8 57	– –	12 41	7 27	– –	– –
10 01	*h*3 38	2 53	9 27	*a*5 20	72.0	.......Exmore..... ♁	8 53	*t*12 04	12 37	7 24	*b*10 11	12 14
10 08	*d*3 45	3 00	9 34	*a*5 27	76.3	....Nassawadox.. ♁	8 45	*t*11 58	12 29	7 14	*b*10 01	12 07
10 16	*h*3 50	3 10	9 44	*a*5 32	79.1	.... Bird's Nest .. ♁	8 37	*t*11 54	12 20	7 06	*b*9 54	12 01
10 22	*d*3 55	3 16	9 50	*a*5 37	81.9	....Machipongo.. ♁	8 31	*t*11 50	12 14	7 00	*b*9 49	11 56
10 26	4 01	3 27	10 00	*l*5 43	86.0	......Eastville.... ♁	8 22	*t*11 45	12 07	6 52	9 42	11 51
10 32	*d*4 06	3 34	10 06	*x*5 50	88.9	.......Cobbs...... ♁	8 16	*t*11 41	12 01	6 46	*r*9 36	11 45
10 37	*d*4 09	3 39	10 12	*a*5 55	90.4	.....**Cheriton**... ♁	8 11	*t*11 39	11 56	6 41	*b*9 31	11 41
10 50	4 20	3 50	10 25	6 05	95.0	arr.} **Cape** {lve.	†8 00	11 30	11 45	†6 30	9 20	11 30
P M	4 30	4 30	A M	6 25	95.0	lve.} **Charles** ♁ {arr.	A M	11 20	11 20	P M	8 55	11 20
.....	6 20	6 20	.....	8 15	119.0	**Old Pt. Comfort**[3]	.....	9 25	9 25	.....	7 00	9 25
.....	7 25	7 25	.....	9 20	131.0	......**Norfolk**[4].....	.....	8 40	8 40		6 00	8 40
.....	7 45	7 45	.....	10 00	.....	ar.**Portsmouth**[5]lv.	.....	†8 00	†8 00	...	*5 00	§8 00
.....	P M	P M	.....	A M	.....	(*High Street.*)	.....	A M	A M	...	P M	A M
P M	P M	....	A M	.....	.....	**CRISFIELD BR.**	A M	P M	.....	P M	.....	.....
†8 07	†2 41	.....	†7 40	.....	21.6	lve. **King's Creek**.arr.	6 45	1 15	.....	7 35	.....	.....
8 12	2 48	.....	7 47	.....	24.4	......Westover ... ♁	6 36	1 05	.....	7 25	.....	.....
8 21	2 56	.....	7 53	.....	28.1	......Kingston.... ♁	6 29	12 58	.....	7 15	.....	.....
8 30	3 04	.....	8 02	.....	31.6	......Marion .... ♁	6 20	12 51	.....	7 05	.....	.....
8 38	3 11	.....	8 09	.....	34.9	......Hopewell.... ♁	6 12	12 45	.....	6 55	.....	.....
8 50	3 25	.....	8 20	.....	38.1	.....**Crisfield**[2]... ♁	†6 00	†12 30	.....	†6 40	.....	.....
P M	P M	.....	A M	.....	.....	ARRIVE] [LEAVE	A M	Noon	.....	P M	.....	.....

Additional Trains—Leaves Pocomoke †6 25 a.m., arrives Delmar 7 50 a.m. Returning, leaves Delmar †10 15 p.m., arrives Pocomoke 11 15 p.m.

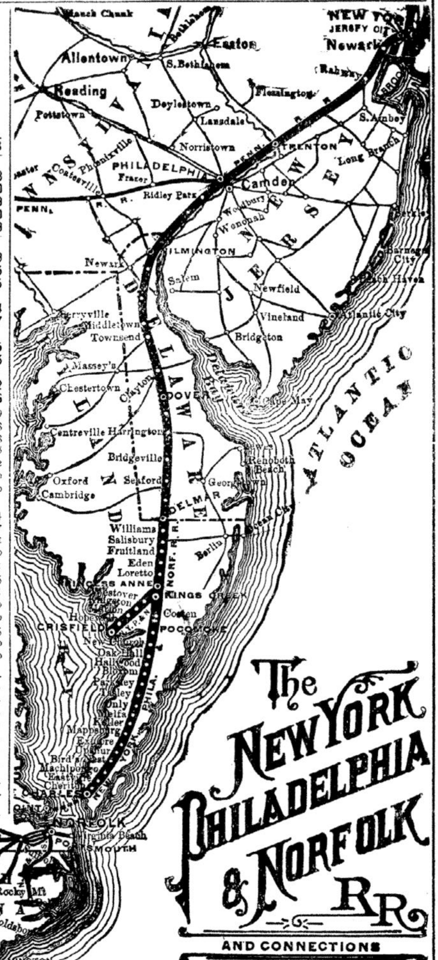

All through tickets of foreign lines' issue convey a stop-over privilege at Old Point Comfort only.

.....	203	201	Mls	CAPE CHARLES R.R.	202	204
.....	P M	A M	....	LEAVE] [ARRIVE	A M	P M
.....	†4 25	†9 30	0	....**Cape Charles**....	11 00	5 55
.....	4 40	9 45	5.1	.... Plantation	10 47	5 40
.....	4 47	9 52	7.4	.......Capeville.......	10 40	5 33
.....	4 52	9 57	8.8	...... Townsend	10 35	5 28
.....	5 05	10 10	12.2	..... **Kiptopeke**	†10 20	†5 15
.....	P M	A M	....	ARRIVE] [LEAVE	A M	P M

STANDARD—*Eastern time.*

Nos. 47 and 48-1048—Broiler Buffet Parlor Car between Philadelphia and Cape Charles. **Nos. 49 and 50**—Steel Sleeping Cars and Passenger Coaches between New York, Philadelphia and Cape Charles. Philadelphia Sleeping Car open at 10 00 p.m. in Broad St. Station. Berths retainable in Philadelphia Sleeping Car until 7 00 a.m.

Through Trains run to and from Pennsylvania Station, 7th Ave. and 32d Street, New York City.

*Daily; †daily, except Sunday; *a* stops to take for Old Point Comfort, Norfolk and Portsmouth, and to leave from Wilmington and points beyond; *b* stops to let off from Old Point Comfort, Norfolk and Portsmouth and to take for Wilmington and points beyond; *c* stops to take passengers for New York; *d* stops week-days to leave from Wilmington and points beyond and will make "*a*" stop on Sunday; *e* stops to leave from New York; *h* stops to leave passengers from Wilmington and points beyond on week-days, and will make regular stop on Sunday; *l* makes "*a*" stop on week-days and will make regular stop on Sunday; *r* makes "*b*" stop on Sunday, will not stop on week-days; *t* stops to take for Wilmington and points beyond; *x* makes "*a*" stop on Sunday and will not stop on week-days. • Will not stop on Sunday. ♁ Telegraph stations.

CONNECTIONS.—[1] With P. B. & W. R.R. [2] With B. C. & A. Ry. [3] With C. & O. and James River and local steamboat lines. [4] With N. & W. Ry. Norf. So. R.R., A. C. L. R.R., So. Ry., Virginian Ry. and C. & O. Ry. (no transfer between N. Y. P. & O. and C. & O.). [5] With S. A. L. Ry. (no transfer).

By 1914, the New York, Philadelphia and Norfolk Railroad had nearly double the number of stations on the line. An express line had been added to speed travelers on their journey. During one season, the line had even experimented with Pullman Sleeper Cars that would be placed directly onto the car barges so the travelers could sleep through the entire journey and arrive in Norfolk in luxury.

Makemie Park, Virginia, was originally called Pocomoke Farm. The area was renamed when it became a historical area. The site was the location of the home and family cemetery of Francis Makemie (1658-1708), acknowledged as a founding leader of Presbyterianism in America. The site includes a marker built in 1907 from building bricks and cemetery wall remnants found in the area. The station was constructed about four miles from the site of the historical area. [*Courtesy of the Eastern Shore Railway Museum*]

Parksley was a planned community, again founded as a stop on the railroad. The town father was Henry R. Bennett, a traveling salesman from Delaware, who saw the possibility of a thriving town at this rail stop. Bennett purchased 160 acres from farmer Benjamin Parks, and named the town after the former landowner. His vision was correct. Soon the town was a major shipping point for agricultural goods. [*Courtesy of the Eastern Shore Railway Museum*]

An unknown worker is captured on a maintenance car near Parksley in the 1920s. While many locals went to work for the railroads, it was not uncommon for men to move from the larger cities, such as Philadelphia, to these smaller communities, to raise their families and work for the company. Land was cheap and there was lots of it for sale. [*Courtesy of the Eastern Shore Railway Museum*]

In 1899, the Eastern Shore of Virginia Produce Exchange was created. The reason was to market potatoes cooperatively, to standardize the product and broaden the outlet. It began to function in the year 1900, little dreaming that in a few years with the hearty cooperation of the growers of this district, it would dominate the potato industry of the country as it did for a large number of years. During the period of 1900 to 1910, production increased rapidly. The records for the year 1910 disclose the railroad moved, from this district alone, 1,606,206 barrels of Irish potatoes and 907,766 barrels of sweet potatoes. [*Courtesy of the Eastern Shore Railway Museum*]

The Delmarva Peninsula, specifically the lower eastern shore of Maryland and Virginia, was the most highly specialized strawberry district in the world in the early 1900s. The area was considered the world's basket for the best strawberries grown anywhere on the globe. As such, shippers from all over America came to the area to purchase the sweet crop. Here, local farmers wait their turn at Onley to load their cargo onto ice-cold boxcars. [*Courtesy of the Eastern Shore Railway Museum*]

Melfa, Virginia, was another of the railroad created communities. A father and his young son pose to have their picture taken at the center of their town. The community was named after one of the railway officials. As with so many other stops on the line, these small communities thrived as the railroad grew. [*Courtesy of the Eastern Shore Railway Museum*]

After the N.Y. P. & N. purchased the Crisfield Branch, the line also saw a spike in business. Seafood was soon being shipped all over the United States, and Crisfield became known as the "Seafood Capital of the World." Crisfield became the second largest city in Maryland, with the population topping off at about 25,000 during the boom, with people from as far as New England and the Midwest. With the help of the railroad, the city set records for shipping seafood which still stand today, shipping the most shucked oysters in one day (1920), shipping twenty-nine train carloads of fish in one day (1922), shipping 1.5 million soft crabs in one day (1928), and shipping 20,000 gallons of crab meat in one day (also 1928).

Before the warning bell and crossing gates were invented, motorists had to be warned about the train coming to a crossing. Thus, railroads employed men to be watchman. Their jobs included stopping traffic at crossings. As the train approached, they would walk into the center of the road with their stop sign. Here, Herbert Hall of Cape Charles, Virginia, shows his job to a photographer. At some crossings on Delmarva, these men worked until the 1940s. [*Courtesy of the Cape Charles Historical Society*]

The Watchman's shack was the building he would be stationed in while guarding his assigned crossing. This particular shack was located in Cape Charles, Virginia, and Hall may have worked this location. In the winter, a small potbelly stove kept the small shack warm, and in the summer, all the workman could hope for was a nice breeze. [*Courtesy of the Cape Charles Historical Society*]

A group of workmen are taking a break from their jobs when this picture was taken. The carts shown are for carting the luggage of passengers traveling both by train and ferry. It took large numbers of employees to maintain and run the railroad. With all the exposure to salt water and frequent tidal flooding, it took a small army to keep the trains and ferries running and on schedule. [*Courtesy of the Cape Charles Historical Society*]

The office staff at Cape Charles had the daunting task of keeping the travelers and freight moving through the busy port in the 1920s. Pictured from left to right: 1st row, H. D. Travis, Frances Detwiler, C. H. Hudson, W. H. Mapp, C. I. Gaskill, Nell Harrington, B. B. Stevenson, A. F. Dize, John Baugh, Milton Stevenson, and H. W. Layfield; 2nd row, standing, Dr. Hunter (Medical Examiner), V. C. Taylor, J. L. Warren, Minnie Disharoon, Gladys Johnson, H. L. Stanbridge, I. J. Burbage, I. L. Swann, G. W. Curtiss, E. J. Hunt, J. J. Restein, E. T. Warner, H. J. Esham, M. E. Culver, J. D. King, H. K. Lockhart, Etta Mercer, Lola Churn, J. W. Dillahunt, and J. H. Powell. [*Courtesy of the Cape Charles Historical Society*]

With such a large number of employees, some of them would join sports leagues as a form of recreation. Here, the New York, Philadelphia and Norfolk Baseball team is ready for a game. Baseball leagues formed all over the Eastern Shore and most towns had a home team. Several players would later become professional baseball players. [*Courtesy of the Cape Charles Historical Society*]

The "Elisha Lee" was one of the railroad's favorite vessels. Originally built for the New Haven Steamboat Company in 1892, the ferry would come to carry a record number of passengers for the company until it ceased service in 1953. The ship was given the honor of carrying the last passengers that would cross the channel to Norfolk via the ferry line. [*Courtesy of the Cape Charles Historical Society*]

By the early 1960s, freight travel had rapidly declined. Cars once were hauled thirty at a time, but as the photo shows, the average was now twelve cars. With the building of a major highway and the Chesapeake Bay Bridge Tunnel, trucks had begun transporting the bulk of the freight now traveling overland. [*Courtesy of Keith Short & Jim Bowden*]

CAPE CHARLES RAILROAD.

In Effect 12.01 A. M. August 6, 1911.

SOUTHWARD.						NORTHWARD.				
2d Class. 203 Lv. Daily ex. Sun. P. M.	2d Class. 201 Lv. Daily ex. Sun. A. M.	Capacity of Freight Sidings.	Distance Between Stations.	Distance from End of Double Track.	STATIONS.	Telephone • Day Office.	Distance from Townsend.	Distance Between Stations.	2d Class. 202 Ar. Daily ex. Sun. A. M.	2d Class. 204 Ar. Daily ex. Sun. P. M.
4.36	9.36				CAPE JUNCTION (SO. E. D. T.)		6.7	3.0	10.40	5.40
s 4.45	s 9.50	25	3.0	3.0	PLANTATION	D	3.7	2.3	s10.32	s 5.27
s 4.52	s10.00	25	2.3	5.3	CAPEVILLE	D	1.4	1.4	s10.25	s 5.17
s 4.57	s10.05	25	1.4	6.7	TOWNSEND	D			s10.20	s 5.10
P. M. 203 Ar. Daily ex. Sun.	A. M. 201 Ar. Daily ex. Sun.								A. M. 202 Lv. Daily ex. Sun.	P. M. 204 Lv. Daily ex. Sun.

Train 201 is superior to train No. 202. Train 203 is superior to train No. 204.

Cape Charles Railroad was constructed in the early 1900s to connect the communities south of Cape Charles to the port. Within a few years, the rail line would come under the N.Y. P. & N. Ironically, in 1951, the ferry service would be moved to the endpoint of this branch line, Kiptopeke State Park. This allowed for a shorter and more direct route to and from Norfolk.

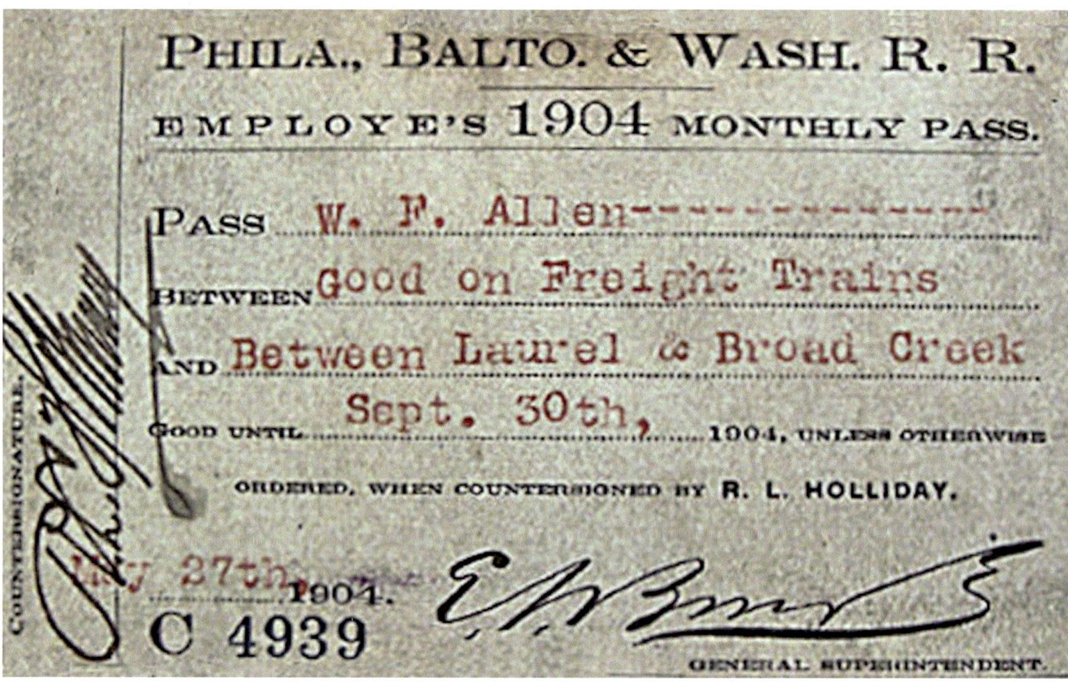
PHILA., BALTO. & WASH. R. R.
EMPLOYE'S 1904 MONTHLY PASS.
PASS W. F. Allen------------
BETWEEN Good on Freight Trains
AND Between Laurel & Broad Creek
GOOD UNTIL Sept. 30th, 1904, UNLESS OTHERWISE ORDERED, WHEN COUNTERSIGNED BY R. L. HOLLIDAY.
COUNTERSIGNATURE.
May 27th 1904.
C 4939
GENERAL SUPERINTENDENT.

Georgetown, Delaware, was always a major stop for the railroads no matter who owned the line. The large water tower and coal chute for loading of water and coal onto the locomotives demonstrates just how large this yard was. Georgetown also was an interchange for trains moving in all four directions, allowing for passengers and freight alike to be transferred to their final destinations.

PREVIOUS PAGE:

Below: In 1902, a major shift occurred on the Delmarva Peninsula. This change actually began back in 1881 when the Pennsylvania Railroad purchased controlling interest in the Philadelphia, Wilmington and Baltimore Railroad. The board of directors of every line control by the P. W. & B. was stacked with men whose focus was on aligning these smaller railroads with the PRR time schedules and the sharing of business opportunities. A new corporation was created with these lines brought under the new company's control: The Delaware Railroad, Cambridge & Seaford Railroad, Queen Anne's & Kent Railroad, and the Delaware & Chesapeake Railroad. Later, the Baltimore & Delaware Bay Railroad was brought in, and the Baltimore and Potomac with its smaller short lines also became a part of this new conglomerate. The Philadelphia, Baltimore and Washington Railroad was born. The line ran from Armstrong, Delaware, to Pocomoke, Maryland, where it interchanged with the N. Y. P. & N. Railroad.

The western parts of lower Delaware were renowned for growing some of the sweetest watermelons in the United States. Laurel, Delaware, grew and shipped such large crops that by the 1940s an auction house had been set up and nearly every melon sold in Delaware commercially was processed and purchased through this location, with buyers from supermarkets across the East Coast. This photo from 1905 shows the P. W. & B. cars loading the juicy fruit onto boxcars. [*Courtesy of the Delaware Public Archives*]

NEXT PAGE:

Above: Not all train lines were built for permanent work. Here a narrow-gauge line was constructed to help with road construction in Laurel, Delaware. Running right down the middle of the street, construction supplies and equipment could be brought directly to the site. Major highway construction across Delmarva used these lines until the 1940s. [*Courtesy of the Delaware Public Archives*]

Below: Selbyville, Delaware, had been a stop as early as the Frankford and Breakwater Railroad. Now with the P.B. & W. the station was another busy freight and passenger depot. Again, strawberries were king here. The fruit would be shipped all over the east coast, resulting in the area joining the rest of the lower Delmarva Peninsula as the strawberry supplier of America.

The Philadelphia Baltimore and Washington connected with the New York, Philadelphia and Norfolk Railroad in Salisbury, as did the Baltimore, Chesapeake and Atlantic. However, the P. W. & B. would use the swing bridge over the Pocomoke River to travel further south to pick up passengers and freight. Here the swing bridge is shown prior to Cassatt Tower being built, around 1900.

The time had come to bring everyone in and place the railroads of Delmarva under the parent company. In 1922, the New York, Philadelphia and Norfolk Railroad was merged into the PRR family. Two branches were established under the PRR. The Delaware Division had its headquarters in Clayton, Delaware, while the Norfolk Division was based out of Cape Charles, Virginia. In 1930, the two were combined into the Delmarva Division of the PRR. Passengers could now board in New York City and travel to their final destination on board the Pennsylvania Railroad.

With the full takeover by the Pennsylvania Railroad, the lines of Delmarva saw larger equipment servicing the line than ever before. Passenger trains routinely were twelve cars long, and freight trains could easily be fifty cars or more. Gone were the days of sleepy small towns on Delmarva. The PRR now dominated the railroad industry.

Blackbird, Delaware, was a small station along the railway since the first lines were built by the Delaware Railroad. The town actually had a long history of being a stagecoach passenger stop and even according to local lore, a port for Blackbeard the pirate for storing booty along the nearby creek. [*Courtesy of the Delaware Public Archives*]

Bellevue Interlocking Block Tower stood watch over the busy Wilmington, Delaware, interchanges for decades. This tower witnessed the growth and then the demise of the Pennsylvania Railroad. The electric lines in the photograph show the changeover for passenger service from coal to electric engines, which were cheaper to operate. These lines were put into place in 1928. [*Courtesy of Ed Kline*]

Inside the Bellevue Tower, you can see the early method used to throw a rail line switch. These large levers would be attached to a series a bars and gears, traveling down from the second story to the ground level, then, like an octopus, branching out in many directions. These heavy bars had to be kept well lubricated, as did the switches themselves in order for the operator to move the lever. [*Courtesy of Ed Kline*]

As train size and speed increased, the safety of those awaiting the train would become an ever-growing concern. Here at Edgemoor, Delaware, a fence had been installed to keep people back from the closely passing trains. [*Courtesy of Ed Kline*]

Delmar, Delaware, was for a few years the end of the line for the Delaware Railroad. Due to this, a large yard and engine repair facility was constructed in the town. In fact, the town was named for the two states it straddles, Delaware and Maryland. The yard workers proudly pose with their newest engine from the Pennsylvania Railroad.

One of the major interchanges among several of the railroads was located in Georgetown, Delaware. This Sussex County town had been a hub for commerce long before the railroad, even having been built around a circle at its center, so the town seemed destined for this event. Goods and passengers could choose from three different train services to travel to their destinations. [*Courtesy of the Delaware Public Archives*]

New Castle, Delaware, was the home of the first railroad of Delaware, but by the early 1900s, it was now just a small stop along the line. While passenger service was certainly still a large part of the railroad business, the city of Wilmington had now become the busy shipping port and most commercial businesses had relocated there as well. [*Courtesy of the Delaware Public Archives*]

Oxford, Maryland, was at one time the water connection for the Maryland and Delaware railroad. The terminal and wharf were completed in 1871. The port town was a hub for a bounty of seafood including crabs, oysters and crabs. Following the coming of the railroad, the town saw a huge boom as several packing houses sprang up to take advantage of the terminal wharf and shipping opportunities. [*Courtesy of the Oxford Museum*]

Milford, Delaware, had for a long time been a major ship building community. When the Delaware Railroad was proposed, they lobbied very vocally to make sure the line came to their town directly. When they and their nearby shipping neighbor Frederica, were bypassed, they even proposed their own railroad to connect the two port cities. Soon, however, Milford got the railroad with the Junction and Breakwater. Edward Chapman served as a watchman in the community for several years. [*Courtesy of the Delaware Public Archives*]

During each World War, the railroad saw large increases in both passenger and freight traffic. Moving the men and materials for war, especially World War II, took a herculean effort. During both wars, the federal government took over the scheduling and movements of the railroad industry to facilitate these efforts. Princess Anne passenger station sends off our heroes during a World War I rally.

Princess Anne, Maryland, was another town that became the county seat and with the government's movement there, business and homeowners followed. The city also was near both agricultural and seafood ports, so goods were brought to the station for shipping to the major cities of the country. The station was one of the last to cease passenger service in the 1950s.

Redden, Delaware, was another of those small farming community stops on the railroad. The community actually dated back to the early 1700s and was a very busy timber area in the state. So when the train came through, it was natural that this small crossroads got a station. But as with so many, not long after the PRR took control, the passenger station was closed.

The Pennsylvania Railroad had a long history of naming their express trains. Here the "Delmarva Express" rolls through the countryside on a snowy day in January 1941. This train grew even more important with the start of World War II. You could board a train at 7:30 in the morning and be in Norfolk, Virginia, by 6:30 p.m. that evening. Moving military personnel became a huge portion of the PRR's business.

The United States Postal Service had long used the trains to transport the U.S. Mail. Railroad Post Office, or RPO, was used on almost all passenger trains. These contracts with the Postal Service were a huge source of revenue and one of the main reasons passenger trains continued to run despite the reduction of riders. A mailbag hangs ready for the next passing train to pick up in Viola, Delaware. [*Courtesy of the Delaware Public Archives*]

By the 1950s, most of the Delmarva Peninsula had seen an end to passenger service on the branch lines such as the one serving Easton, Maryland. The freight stations had even a dramatic drop in service. Most of the trains now ran directly to the customer with a small rail siding directly at the shipper's warehouse. The buildings began to be ignored, and as money became tighter, so did the equipment and rails themselves.

The main line down Delmarva continued to see busy seasons. Spring and summer would still see a spike in the number of freight cars traveling the rails, carrying goods to market. But the days of thousands of cars needed to carry the produce had disappeared. A PRR switcher engine works to position a train for pickup on the main line in Seaford, Delaware.

Penn Central Railroad—what is there to say about what is still the one of the largest business failures in American history? By the late 1950s, passenger service had come to an end on most of Delmarva. Freight business was dropping as well. The Pennsylvania Railroad, due to government regulation of the railroad industry, was struggling to survive, as was most of the railroad industry in America. So in January of 1968, the unthinkable happened.

The once mighty Pennsylvania Railroad merged with its once bitter rival and another giant of the railroad industry, the New York Central Railroad. At the time of the merger it created a monster of over 20,000 miles of railroad that devoured operating costs of 5 million dollars a day. While the line boasted service to the lucrative Northeast, it also had so many routes that were unprofitable, the Penn Central bled cash from day one.

While the main line of the old Delaware Railroad still saw brisk traffic, passenger service, which had once been so profitable for the old lines, fell to the point it was no longer feasible to continue. Even the service on the Metroliners between major cities such as Philadelphia and Washington was nearly discounted due to those lines losing money.

The coal train headed to the Indian River Power Plant run by Delmarva Power was one of the few guaranteed sites on Delmarva even during the lean times of the Penn Central. The plant at the time was coal powered and it was common to see this train pulling forty or more cars of coal south twice a week to keep the lights on in the towns of Delmarva. Today, the plant uses mostly oil-fired turbines so the days of the long coal trains have ended.

Finally, on June 21, 1970, the Penn Central reached the end of the line and bankruptcy was declared. Sadly, the railroad never really stood a chance. Archaic business models, infighting, governmental regulation, and poor cost controls over equipment and labor had doomed the venture from the start. But from the ashes a new phoenix arose. It took time, government deregulation, and new ways of doing business, but the darkness of what is viewed as the worst times of the railroad industry began to lift. *[Courtesy of Dom Cataldi]*

Amtrak was the first railroad organized by the Federal Government following the collapse of Penn Central. The company is actually called the National Passenger Railroad Corporation. The line has been subsidized by the federal government since its inception and despite efforts to change this, it appears that there will always be a need for government assistance in the area of passenger service on the railroads. Here, a passenger train stops at the renovated Joe Biden Station in Wilmington, Delaware.

Traveling south from Wilmington, Amtrak still runs over lines completed decades ago by the Delaware and Pennsylvania Railroad. Just south of the location shown in this photograph is one of the many Amtrak yards in the Northeast. (Courtesy of Mark Glucksman).

Today, there is only one passenger station south of Wilmington to board a train today: Newark, Delaware. Here, the Acela line, Amtrak's newest high-speed passenger service, awaits to depart. A new station is being built to serve the area, but it is certainly a far cry from the hundreds of passenger stations that once dotted the Delmarva landscape.

The Southeastern Pennsylvania Transportation Authority (SEPTA) was created by the Pennsylvania legislature on August 17, 1963. SEPTA was subsidized by the state of Pennsylvania, taking over the lines of the Reading and Pennsylvania railroads, and again adding the Penn Central when Conrail as created. Today, SEPTA services have the sixth largest U.S. rapid transit system by ridership, and the fifth largest overall transit system. SEPTA is one of only two U.S. transit authorities that operates all of the five major types of terrestrial transit vehicles: regional (commuter) rail trains, "heavy" rapid transit (subway/elevated) trains, light rail vehicles (trolleys), trolleybuses, and motorbuses.

Following the financial collapse of the Penn Central, the federal government stepped in to save the railroad industry. It took a threat from Penn Central in 1973 to totally cease operations for the federal government to take action. The law signed on January 2, 1974, by President Richard Nixon funded the bankrupt lines while creating the Consolidated Rail Corporation, or as it came to be called Conrail. Here, the bright blue colors of Conrail can be seen at the yard in Harrington, Delaware. [*Courtesy of Chris Hash*]

In 1974, Penn Central had filed to abandon the old rails between Berlin, Maryland, and West Ocean City, Maryland. However, this was withdrawn when the Historic Railroad Company of Severna, Maryland, negotiated to purchase the line. The Ocean City Western Railroad ran an excursion train on the line until 1976, when that portion of the company ceased operating. The line continued with minimal freight service for another ten years, but in 1987, the entire line was sold and the tracks removed. [*Courtesy of Stephie Kolata*]

PREVIOUS PAGE:

Below: Conrail's economic recovery and turnaround began in 1980 when the Staggers Rail Act was signed into law deregulating railroads, allowing railroads to become more competitive with trucks. The act allowed them to price services, adjust rail rates, react to market conditions, and provide special contracts. Conrail's first year of profitability came in 1981. By 1983, Conrail was the fourth largest freight hauler in the United States. In 1987, Conrail was returned to the private sector in what was then the largest initial public offering in U.S. history, raising $1.9 billion. In the spring of 1997, Norfolk Southern Corporation (NS) and CSX Corporation (CSX) agreed to acquire Conrail through a joint stock purchase.

Like many areas of the former Penn Central Railroad, the Delmarva Peninsula was not operating at Class One efficiency. In addition to the primary mainline between Wilmington, Delaware, and Pocomoke, Maryland, there were several small branch lines that needed minimal rail service. Many of these lines roamed into some of the most rural areas on the shore, and were simply not fit for a larger carrier. With poor track in continually deteriorating condition, the branches were omitted from the Final System Plan, which created Conrail in 1976 and was slated to be abandoned. However, politicians from the states of Maryland and Delaware contracted with Conrail to operate these struggling branches as a subsidized "designated operator" with ownership retained by Penn Central. After one year of operation, the expense of subsidizing these lines at Conrail's high cost led the state governments to seek a lower cost short line as a "designated operator." In August 1977, the Maryland and Delaware Railroad Company (MDDE) was created. Soon after its organization, the firm was selected as the "designated operator" of three branches in its namesake states. These branches are Centreville, Chestertown, and Seaford Lines. The Seaford Line runs between Seaford, Delaware, and Hurlock, Maryland. The Centreville Line runs between Townsend, Delaware, and Centreville, Maryland. The Chestertown Line runs between Massey and Worton, Maryland. Each of these lines runs the same rail beds their predecessors had used before them. [*Courtesy of Royden Powell*]

NEXT PAGE:

Above: In 1982, the Maryland and Delaware took an opportunity to offer a once-in-a-lifetime excursion train from Easton, Maryland to Clayton, Delaware. Since this train's special trip that day, most of these rails have been removed, with a rails to trails put in their place. Here the train rolls through the town of Goldsboro, Maryland. [*Courtesy of Royden Powell*]

Below: The Maryland and Delaware today frequently partners with the city of Hurlock, Maryland, to run special excursion trains during the city's annual heritage festival. These specialty trains allow people to once again experience the feeling their forefathers lived daily, the riding of the rails, and the clickety-clack of the steel wheels over the tracks. For a day, passenger trains once again roam the Eastern Shore. [*Courtesy of Royden Powell*]

MARYLAND & DELAWARE

MARYLAND & DELAWARE
2628
NORFOLK AND WESTERN

In June of 2019, the Maryland and Delaware returned service to Berlin, Maryland. Local citizens and governmental officials alike were very excited to see the return of the railroad. These trains will serve Delmarva's largest industry today, poultry farming. In 2018, the Delmarva chicken industry produced 605 million birds a year and generated $3.4 billion in value. Approximately seventy-three percent of Delmarva's cash farm income was from meat chickens in 2016. [*Courtesy of the Maryland & Delaware Railroad*]

On April 1, 1977, the Virginia and Maryland Railroad took over the Cape Charles yard after the departure of the Pennsylvania Railroad and Conrail. Conrail had decided the line south of Pocomoke, Maryland, was not economically feasible with the lack of traffic versus the cost of rehabilitating the line. After the company took over the line, extensive track renovation was undertaken. The railroad was headquartered in Cape Charles, Virginia. [*Courtesy of the Eastern Shore Railroad Museum*]

Originally built for the Long Island Railroad, this ALCO C420 was purchased and was used heavily on the line. When it arrived, it was quickly given a logo, the number 200, and pressed into service before it could even visit the paint shop. The line only owned six engines during its time. [*Courtesy of Stephie Kolata*]

The 200 ALCO finally got all dressed up with the official colors of the Virginia and Maryland Railroad. The 200 sister engine, Engine 203, was involved in an incident where it and the car float it was riding sank in the Chesapeake Bay. Once recovered, that engine had to be retired due to damage. Sadly the VAMD could not make a profit from the line and sold its assets in October of 1981. [*Courtesy of Stephie Kolata*]

The Eastern Shore Railroad was the next company to try and make the once vital port of Cape Charles a shipping point again. After buying out the Virginia and Maryland, the company set out to try and increase business on the car ferry line to Norfolk, Virginia. The line had eleven stops between Pocomoke, Maryland, and Cape Charles, Virginia.

The two locomotives were originally purchased by the Illinois Central Railroad and eventually sold to the Eastern Shore Railroad. Both restored, they were considered the best engines the line had in service. However, the line was marginally successful and was once again sold in February 2006. [*Courtesy of David Simmons*]

Bay Coast was the last company to try its hand at Cape Charles, Virginia. The company was organized by a familiar last name, the Cassatt Management, LLC. By the time the company took over, the line was a shell of its former self. Most of the locomotives suffered from various levels of disrepair. Enough of the locomotives were repaired to function, while the rest were sold for scrap. [*Courtesy of Evan Shilling*]

The Bay Coast business by now was mostly freight delivery, utilizing the exchange with Norfolk Southern, which had taken over the Delmarva Region from Conrail. Still using the interchange at Pocomoke, Maryland, business was infrequent for the line, and almost non-existent for the car barge portion.

In 2014, Bay Coast abandoned to car float business. In 2017, the company lost the bulk propane business in Norfolk, Virginia. This was the final bell toll for operations and in May 2018, all railroad operations ceased on the line that once carried millions of tons of goods annually on Delmarva. A few cars and a locomotive were donated to the Cape Charles Museum. The rail yard was scraped and is being sold for development.

The former headquarters for so many people now sits vacant, awaiting the once bustling railroad line's fate. The New York, Philadelphia and Norfolk had transformed Delmarva, particularly the Eastern Shore of Virginia, into an area that was once the most powerful produce growing area in the United States. Small towns saw millions of dollars come into their area in the early 1900s, causing a boom that was greater than any had imagined.

Another short line took over a section of rail in Delaware that Conrail had abandoned. The Delaware Coast Line Railroad operated rail lines that were part of the former Queen Anne's Railroad, which provided the service from Love Point, Maryland, to Lewes, Delaware. The company ran sections of track from Ellendale to Milton, Delaware, and between Georgetown and Lewes, Delaware.

For a few years, the Delaware Coast Line ran an excursion train from Nassau, Delaware, to Lewes, Delaware, utilizing one of the most unique features on the line, one that had existed since 1869. The manual swing bridge crossed over the Lewes and Rehoboth Canal in Lewes. To open and close the bridge, the operator had to hand-crank the structure. The bridge was modernized by PRR in 1916 and reconstructed in 1997. [*Courtesy of Keith Short & Jim Bowden*]

In September 2016, the swing bridge was found to be structurally unsound, having dropped 7-8 inches due to settlement in the canal and split timber pieces. As a result, the bridge was closed to rail traffic by officials. The line then lost the contract to operate the remainder of its line in December of 2017. The line closed and sold off all of its assets. Their former caboose still sits in the abandoned yard at Georgetown, Delaware.

Norfolk Southern was the winner of the bid for Conrail's Delmarva line in 1997, resetting the merger of the Pennsylvania Railroad and New York Central Railroad that created Penn Central. The balance of Conrail was acquired by CSX. Norfolk Southern still faced repair issues that Conrail had not completed, but as a whole the line was in good shape. [*Courtesy of Richard Layne*]

Rolling past the Wyoming Station, a town and station that was created by the coming of the Delaware Railroad in 1855, the Delmarva Region was still profitable, but with limited customers and more short haul trains, Norfolk Southern began to look toward leasing the line to an operator that could provide morc onc on onc customcr scrvicc.

Enter to the scene the newest railroad on Delmarva, Delmarva Central Railroad. The parent corporation is Carload Express, which is based out of Oakmont, Pennsylvania. The line is still owned by Norfolk Southern, and is leased to Carload. This move allowed a company experienced in the short line business to take over the day-to-day operations of the area and give customers more individual attention. [*Courtesy of Nathan Sloski*]

Delmarva Central Railroad chose Harrington, Delaware, for its offices, once again making this railroad hub the center of rail activity in lower Delaware. The line operates several interchanges with Norfolk Southern, The Maryland and Delaware, and CSX, thus allowing the railroad to deliver cargo to business all over Delmarva.

In June 2018, the DCR took over operations from the Bay Coast Railroad following the closure of the line. Abandonment plans have been introduced to remove all rails south of Hallwood, Virginia, DCR's current final stop on the line. Most recently, the DCR took over operations from the Delaware Coast Line Railroad between Ellendale and Milton and Georgetown and Cool Spring, having won the bid to operate the lines under a contract with the State of Delaware.

The streetcar was introduced in America in 1832 in New York City, followed closely by New Orleans, Louisiana. Despite Wilmington, Delaware's small size, they were quick to jump into the streetcar fray. The Wilmington City Railway was incorporated on February 4, 1864. The link was quickly constructed and the first horse-drawn carriage made its maiden run on June 30, 1864. Pictured here (left to right): Dennis Lynch, Driver; James F. Taylor; Unknown Minnick, Painter; J. Dorsey, Blacksmith; On the platform (left to right): Humphrey Lynch, Driver; William Carpenter.

The small car barn for the trolley line was located near the Baltimore & Ohio station on Delaware Avenue in Wilmington. A waiting room for passengers was constructed and the offices for the line were located in the brick structure as well.

A branch line was built soon after the line opened that ran to Rising Sun Village, while the line opened on October 14, 1864. The station was small and service on the line was infrequent. This symbolized the Wilmington City Railway. Little changed and at times service was barley extended after the initial lines were constructed.

Electricity was being tested for streetcars as early as 1885 in such cities as Scranton, Pennsylvania, and Richmond, Virginia. The Wilmington City Railway needed this new technology to expand service over some of the hills that were too steep for horses. So a contract was agreed upon and after many sparks and spats, the first electric car was tested on January 24, 1888. The system was finally ready to run on March 2, 1888, and this photo is from that opening day. [*Courtesy of the Delaware Public Archives*]

The trolley car number 201 was built by Jackson and Sharp of Wilmington, Delaware, in 1896 and was dubbed the "Party Car." The car was luxurious inside and out, with ornate fixtures, velvet individual seats and rattan wicker chairs as well. The car was used for company officials, dignitaries, and special events around the city. [*Courtesy of the Delaware Public Archives*]

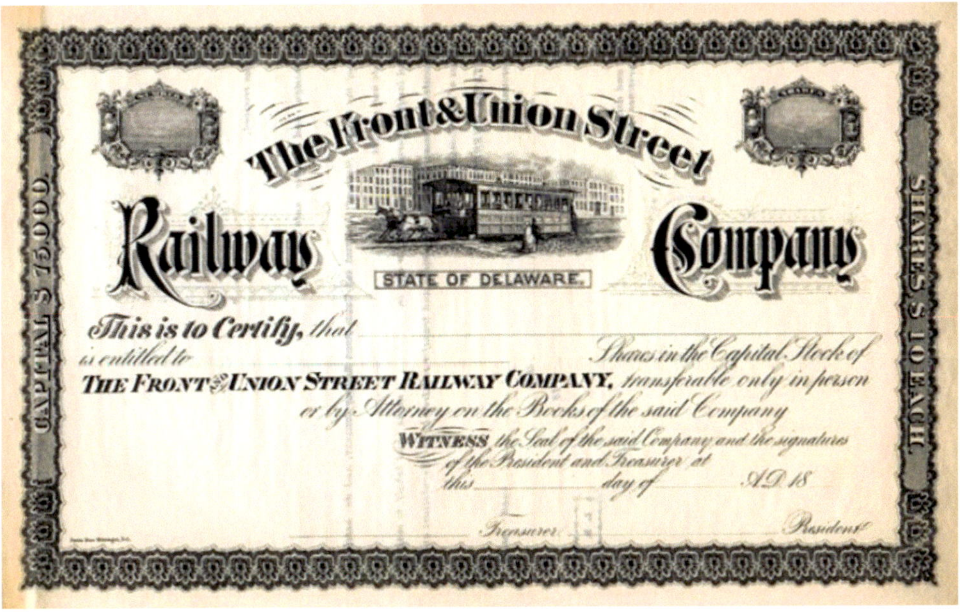

CAPITAL $ 75,000.

The Front & Union Street Railway Company

STATE OF DELAWARE.

SHARES $ 10 EACH.

This is to Certify, that is entitled to Shares in the Capital Stock of THE FRONT & UNION STREET RAILWAY COMPANY, transferable only in person or by Attorney on the Books of the said Company

WITNESS the Seal of the said Company and the signatures of the President and Treasurer at this day of A.D. 18

Treasurer

President

Front & Union Street Railway Company was the next to enter the streetcar scene in Wilmington. The small line began operations on September 11, 1881. The line had limited service but big dreams. They looked into replacing their mules with electricity, expanding to other streets in the city, and even lowered their fares to five cents, just to gain ridership. Competition with the Wilmington Railway was fierce, on both the streets and in the state legislator. Eventually Wilmington City won the war and acquired the Front and Union line in 1891.

No. Shares.

The Gordon Heights Railway Company,

SHARES, $100 EACH.

This Certifies, That is the holder of Shares of the Capital Stock of

THE GORDON HEIGHTS RAILWAY COMPANY,

of the par value of one hundred dollars each, on which has been paid dollars per share. Said shares of stock are transferable only upon the books of the Company, by the stockholder or his duly constituted attorney or representative upon the surrender of this certificate, and under such regulations as may from time to time be established by the by-laws of the Company.

Witness the corporate seal of said Company and the signatures of the President and Treasurer the day of 189

Treasurer. President.

Attest. Secretary.

Gordon Heights began as a feeder line to the Wilmington City Railway. Begun in 1894, the line was built along the then Philadelphia Pike to a pier on the Delaware River. A small amusement park was even constructed to aid in drawing riders to the line. The line was beset with problems, ran intermittently, and was closed in 1903.

INCORPORATED UNDER THE LAWS OF THE STATE OF NEW JERSEY

This Certifies that Howard Rowland is entitled to Forty Shares

OF THE CAPITAL STOCK OF THE

WILMINGTON & CHESTER TRACTION COMPANY

420

transferable only on the books of the Company in person or by Attorney on the surrender of this Certificate. This Certificate is not valid until countersigned by the Transfer Clerk and Registered by the Registrar of Transfers.

SHARES $50 EACH

CANCELLED

Witness the Seal of the Company and the signatures of the President and Treasurer at Camden, N.J.

CAPITAL $2,000,000.

Wilmington & Chester Traction Company was created to bring all of the area's streetcar lines under one roof, from Wilmington to the outskirts of Philadelphia. The company purchased the capital stock for the City Railway, Gordon Heights Railway, Front & Union, and the Chester Traction Company of Pennsylvania.

Wilmington & Chester Car Picture 301 was purchased from Jackson and Sharp in 1900 and placed into service in Wilmington. The company did expand service but suffered from underfunding with the business recession of 1907 only causing the company to suffer financially even further.

INCORPORATED UNDER THE LAWS OF THE STATE OF DELAWARE

Number A213 — 100 Shares

100 Shares

Wilmington and Philadelphia Traction Company

Preferred Stock $1,500,000 — Common Stock $5,000,000

Shares 100 Dollars Each.

This is to Certify that ________ is the owner of ONE HUNDRED Shares of the Common Capital Stock of Wilmington and Philadelphia Traction Company transferable only on the books of the Corporation by the holder hereof in person or by Attorney upon surrender of this Certificate properly endorsed.

In Witness Whereof the said Corporation has caused this Certificate to be signed by its duly authorized officers and to be sealed with the Seal of the Corporation this twenty-eighth day of February A.D. 1911

COMMON

TREASURER — PRESIDENT

Defaulting on payments in 1910, the line was reorganized, and a new group of investors offered up a one-million-dollar preferred stock option, with half subscribed in cash. The new company was formed to manage the lines in Delaware and was named the Wilmington & Philadelphia Traction Company.

Wilmington & Philadelphia was much more successful in managing the operations and the company acquired all other lines in and around Wilmington, Delaware. Once again, all of the lines were run from a single headquarters. Lines ran on time, employees were paid, and fares stabilized. Equipment was finally upgraded and maintained.

Wilmington & Brandywine Springs Railway began in 1893. The Brandywine Springs Park had become so popular that a trolley from the nearby city of Wilmington, Delaware, would make multiple daily trips to and from the park. These trips allowed local service to the park on an even more frequent basis. A local band travels the trolley to perform at the grand opening of the park in the 1890s.

Elsmere & Wilmington Railway was another line that fed trolley riders into the city of Wilmington. Ridership on the line began in August 1897. The line ran a short service to the city's edge, but its charter never allowed for the line to enter the city. It did eventually negotiate rights to connect and run trains to the P. W. & B. station, but it was too little too late. The line was bought by the Wilmington and Brandywine Springs Railway just nine months after it opened in May 1898.

While all those buyouts, bankruptcies, and reorganizations occurred, another trolley line entered into the streetcar business of Wilmington. The People's Railway began on April 23, 1900. The man behind this venture, Richard Crook, was the same man that was the backer of the Brandywine Springs Amusement Park. He set out to build on any street that did not have a trolley in Wilmington, bypassing the monopoly the City Railway had. He brought the W & BS and the E & W under the new company and was able to directly compete with City Railway.

The People's Railway operated probably one of the most unique trolley cars ever in the United States. New Castle County requested the car only be used for hauling its prisoners from the prison to the courthouse and back. So for five years, the car ran four trips each morning and two in the afternoon, Monday through Friday, hauling only inmates from the facility. People's, however, would not last and was purchased by the Wilmington and Philadelphia Traction Company in 1915.

Donald Mallick, ("Happy") was a nine-year-old entrepreneur in 1910, selling newspapers by jumping from car to car. He averaged 35 cents a week in earnings When he was first interviewed he gave a story of sleeping in broken buildings and lots at night. He was often found out in streets at 11 p.m. pitching pennies and working "last paper" schemes. He was also known to flip cars and had a sister who was eight years of age who begged and sold papers as well.

On November 16, 1927, Wilmington & Philadelphia Traction Co. changed its name to the Delaware Electric Power Company, which acted as a holding company for numerous street railway lines, bus companies, and utilities companies in the greater Wilmington region. As electric street railway systems faced continuous competition from gas-powered buses and automobiles throughout the 1920s and 1930s, Delaware Electric Power Co. began to phase out its streetcar system in favor of bus lines and trackless trolleys. [*Courtesy of the Delaware Public Archives*]

By April 1938, the entire line had become trackless. Electric buses now used the overhead wires to power their engines, but rubber wheels now took the place of trolley trucks. Cheaper and more efficient, the cars saved the company money but with more and more transportation options, the line was slowly losing riders. On June 27, 1941, the company once again changed its name to the Delaware Coach Company and the electric generating portion was spun off to become Delaware Electric Company, the largest supplier of power in the state of Delaware today. Finally the last run of the trolley in Delaware came on December 6, 1957. [*Courtesy of the Delaware Public Archives*]

Wilmington & New Castle Electric Railway line was more of a feeder line to the City Railway than a real standalone service to New Castle County. The company began services on February 6 1897. The company was never able to expand beyond its original service lines.

One of the roadblocks encountered by the Wilmington & New Castle Railway was the crossings it was required to build with steam railroad lines in the area. The bridge here was located on Wilmington Road near the trolley barn in New Castle. Stories abounded of passengers too afraid to cross the bridge on the trolley cars, so the trolley would stop, let them walk along the rail lines, then re-board the trolley on the other side of the bridge.

Wilmington & Southern Traction Company was organized in 1911 to take control of the W & NC Electric Railway in hopes that they could extend services further in to New Castle County and possibly all the way to the state capital of Dover, Delaware. However, a separate company, the New Castle & Delaware City Traction Company, had taken over the right to this trolley line. [*Courtesy of the Delaware Public Archives*]

No. 87

Incorporated under the laws of the State of Delaware

Shares.

Wilmington New Castle & Delaware City Railway Company

Full Paid and Non-Assessable

Capital Stock $250,000

This is to certify that ______ is the owner of ______ Shares of the Capital Stock of Wilmington New Castle & Delaware City Railway Company transferable only on the books of the Company by the holder hereof in person or by duly authorized Attorney upon surrender of this Certificate properly endorsed.

Witness the seal of the Company and the signatures of its duly authorized Officers affixed this ______ day of ______ 191

Treasurer

President

Shares 100 Each

The next on the scene and the company that was able to finally untie the lines south of Wilmington was the Wilmington, New Castle & Delaware City Railway. An outside company had purchased the NC & BC, and wanted to combine it with the Wilmington & Southern Traction. After the purchase of that line, the company was involved in many new technologies regarding battery-powered cars. These proved unsuccessful and the line collapsed in 1915. All of it was purchased by the Wilmington and Philadelphia Traction Company in 1915, finally bringing all trolley lines in Delaware under their control.

The old city of Odessa, Delaware, had been bypassed by the Delaware railroad in 1856. A railroad line was originally charted in 1873 to connect Odessa with the station at Middletown, Delaware. Nothing was done until 1891 when a local man, William R. Polk, became obsessed with the electric railway. But he was unable to accomplish his goal. Then he was contacted in 1902 by E. R. Cochran Jr., who said he could get the line done. By August 13, 1903, he kept his word as the first car ran on the line. But the line never saw a profit nor did it employ the mechanics that could even service the cars. It last operated in the fall of 1907.

Eleutherian Mills was the famous gunpowder company that was opened by the DuPont family and was located on the Brandywine River in New Castle County Delaware. Alfred I DuPont was the president of the company and an avid engineer. The mill had its own railroad to move raw materials and product around the sprawling complex. Alfred designed a traction engine in 1905 to work at the mill. [*Courtesy of the Hagley Museum*]

Since the production of gunpowder was very dangerous, the small narrow-gauge line was actually wooden rails, so moving the cargo would not create a spark. Here workers are transporting the fine powder to the packing facility for final preparation before leaving the plant. During the company history, there were a total of 288 explosions, resulting in deaths of 228 people. [*Courtesy of the Hagley Museum*]

Once the final product was placed in wooden barrels for shipping (again, all about safety), the barrels would again be moved by wooden rail to the railroad yard. Only here were metal rails and wheels allowed. The powder would be loaded and shipped to its final destination. The DuPont Powder Works produced most of America's gunpowder supply for the War of 1812 and for the Union during the Civil War. [*Courtesy of the Hagley Museum*]

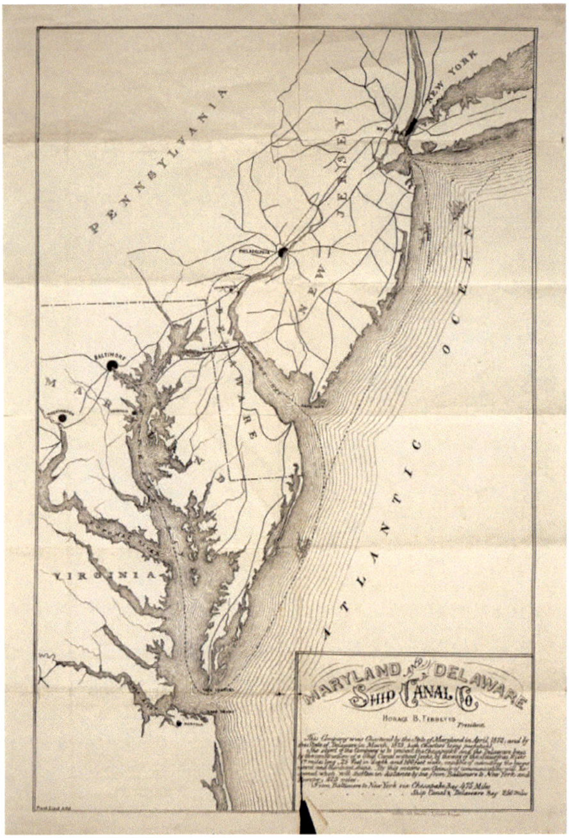

Maryland & Delaware Ship Canal received its charter from the State of Maryland in 1872 and from the State of Delaware in 1873. Its purpose was "to connect the Chesapeake and Delaware bays by construction of a Ship Canal without locks, by the way of the Sassafras River 17 miles long, 25 feet in depth and 100 feet wide, capable of admitting the largest naval and merchant ships." By this means, the builders thought to "shorten the distance by sea from Baltimore to New York and Europe, 225 miles." This new canal was to differ from the existing Chesapeake and Delaware Canal to its northwest, in that it would be constructed without locks, be deeper and wider, allowing deeper draft vessels to travel its length, and cost less to run and maintain. While attractive in thought, the canal was never built.

The New York, Philadelphia and Norfolk Railroad initially owned the ferry operation at Cape Charles, Virginia. Shown here are two of her early vessels, possibly the "Maryland" and "New York," tied up at the Cape Charles Terminal. The line would see several vessels in service over its lifetime, hauling often over 1,000 people per day during the summer months.

In 1934, the Pennsylvania Railroad created a new company to operate the ferry line. The company was named after its sister operation, the New York, Philadelphia and Norfolk Railroad Ferry Company.

In 1933, another company, the Virginia Ferry Corporation, was organized to operate a ferry across the Chesapeake Bay from Cape Charles to Little Creek in Princess Anne County. It leased from the Pennsylvania Railroad Company terminal facilities at each end of the line, Cape Charles and Norfolk, Virginia. In 1949, the terminal at Cape Charles was moved to Kiptopeke, several miles south of Cape Charles. During the 1950s, newer ships were placed into service that could haul passenger cars and trucks. In 1964, with the opening of the Chesapeake Bay Bridge and Tunnel, the ferry service came to a close.

New Castle Manufacturing Company was one of the earliest locomotive manufactures in the United States. The company built the first American manufactured locomotive for the New Castle and Frenchtown Railroad. In 1848, the company produced a locomotive for the Baltimore & Ohio Railroad that was nicknamed the "Old Warhorse." Today, this locomotive has been restored and resides at the B&O Museum in Baltimore, Maryland. The company closed in 1857. [*Courtesy of the New Castle County Historical Society*]

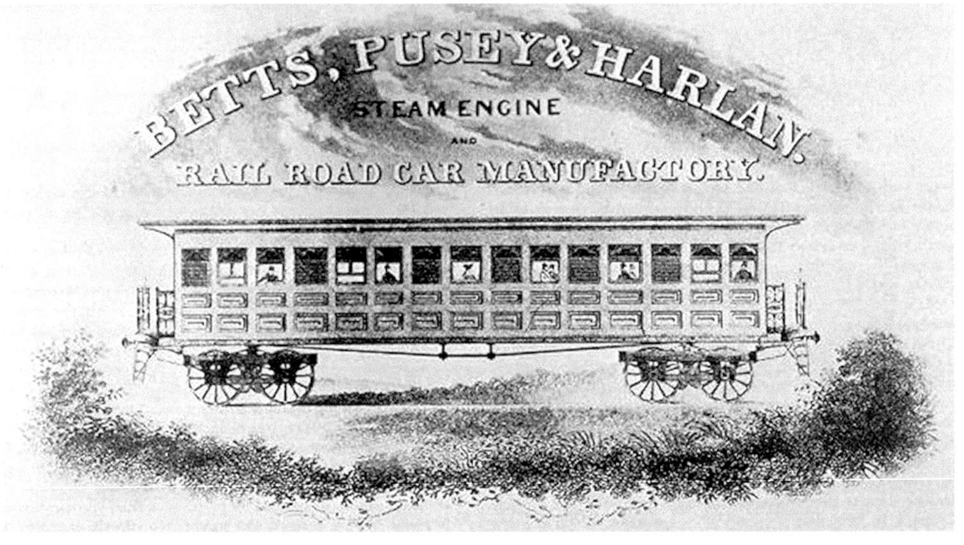

The Betts, Pusey & Harlan Rail Car Company was founded in 1836 by Mahlon Betts and Samuel N. Pusey in Wilmington, Delaware. With the addition of Samuel Harlan shortly thereafter, the firm became known as Betts, Pusey and Harlan. In 1841, Elijah Hollingsworth bought Samuel Pusey's interest in the company. The firm then became known as Betts, Harlan & Hollingsworth, which it would remain until 1849, when Betts withdrew from the firm. Early on the company earned a reputation of producing some of the highest quality railroad locomotives and railcars in the world.

From 1849 to 1858, the company built rail cars and iron ships under the name Harlan & Hollingsworth. The plant grew rapidly during these years as they began to export their products to countries all around the Western Hemisphere. It was one of the first shipbuilding companies in the country to have a foundry.

An interior view of Harlan & Hollingsworth parlor car manufactured in 1881, containing ten sections in an interior of crimson plush, Brussels carpet and "highly polished" French black walnut panels. It was used by the Milwaukee Road on its Pioneer Limited between Chicago and St Paul. [*Courtesy of the Delaware Public Archives*]

The interior of the cars shows both the trend of Victorian Style that was prevalent during the period, but also demonstrates the opulence of these types of cars during the time. Railroads frequently ordered higher end parlor cars for their passengers that wished to travel in luxury. [*Courtesy of the Delaware Public Archives*]

The Jackson & Sharp company was founded in 1863 by Job H. Jackson, a tinsmith and retail merchant, and Jacob F. Sharp, a carpenter who had worked for Harlan and Hollingsworth. They constructed the plant along the mouth of the Brandywine Creek and named the facility the Delaware Car Works. [*Courtesy of the Delaware Public Archives*]

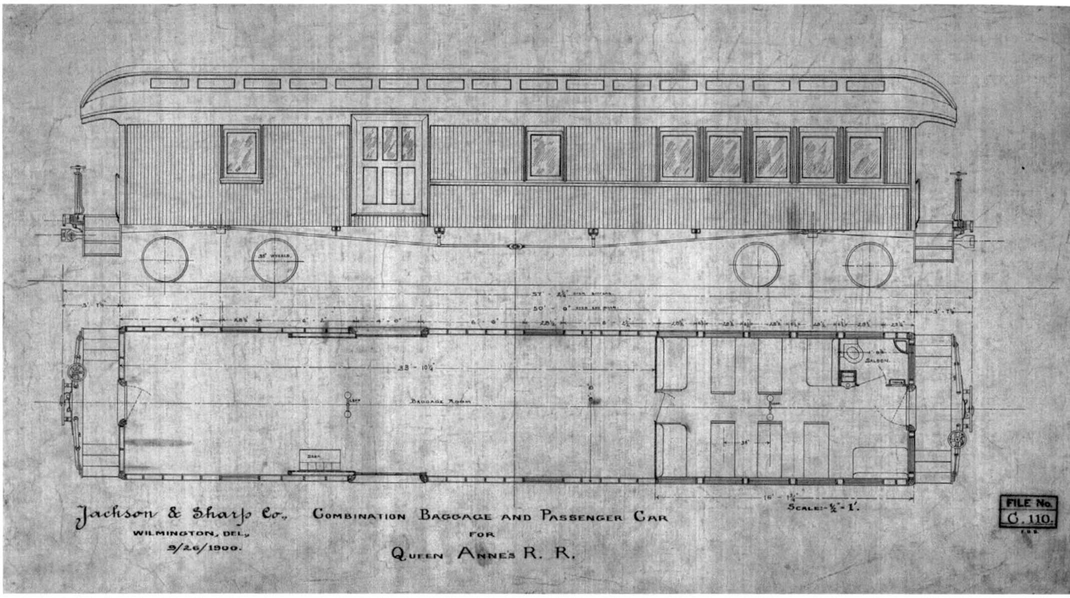

Within twenty years, Jackson & Sharp's capacity grew to seventy-five cars, with about 1,000 employees. At that time, it was considered to be the largest rolling stock plant in the Americas. Despite such close neighbors with Harlan & Hollingsworth, both companies flourished. The drawing for a combination car to be produced for one of Delmarva's own Railroads, the Queen Anne's, shows the company's high-end designs. [*Courtesy of the Delaware Public Archives*]

The exterior of the same car is shown in the drawing that was manufactured for the Queen Anne's Railroad. The car was one of their more "common" cars. Annually, expositions would be held to show off the latest designs of passenger cars, and Jackson and Sharp would become no stranger to winning first place in these shows. The company was well known for its parlor cars produced for King Oscar of Sweden and Dom Pedro, Emperor of Brazil. [*Courtesy of the Delaware Public Archives*]

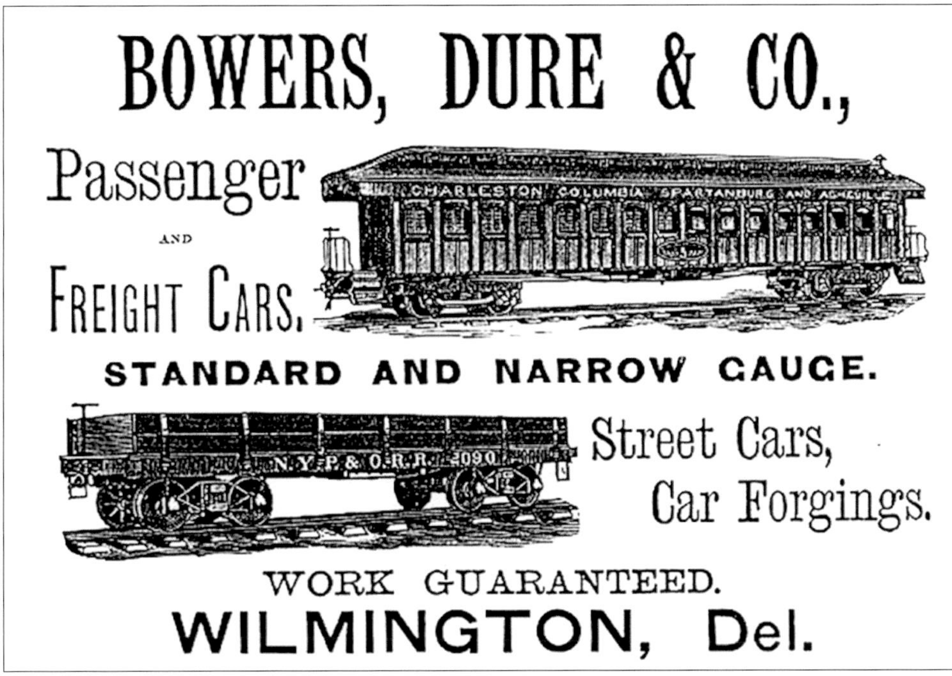

Bowers, Dure & Company was founded in 1871 at Wilmington, Delaware, as a partnership between Thomas Wesley Bowers and Henry F. Dure. The plant was constructed on the Brandywine River alongside the tracks of the Philadelphia, Wilmington & Baltimore Railroad. By 1880, the Wilmington Car Works occupied 21 acres and employed 350, and was considered one of the most modern of its time. They also manufactured ships.

Bowers retired in the early 1880s, and the firm became Dure Car Manufacturing Company. Dure began to specialize in manufacturing for the Pullmans Palace Car Company, and in August of 1886, sold the works to them for $55,000. Pullman would continue to use the factory as their eastern branch repair facility, producing and repairing high-quality passenger cars. The former Bowers, Dure works was still in operation for Pullman at least as late as 1957.

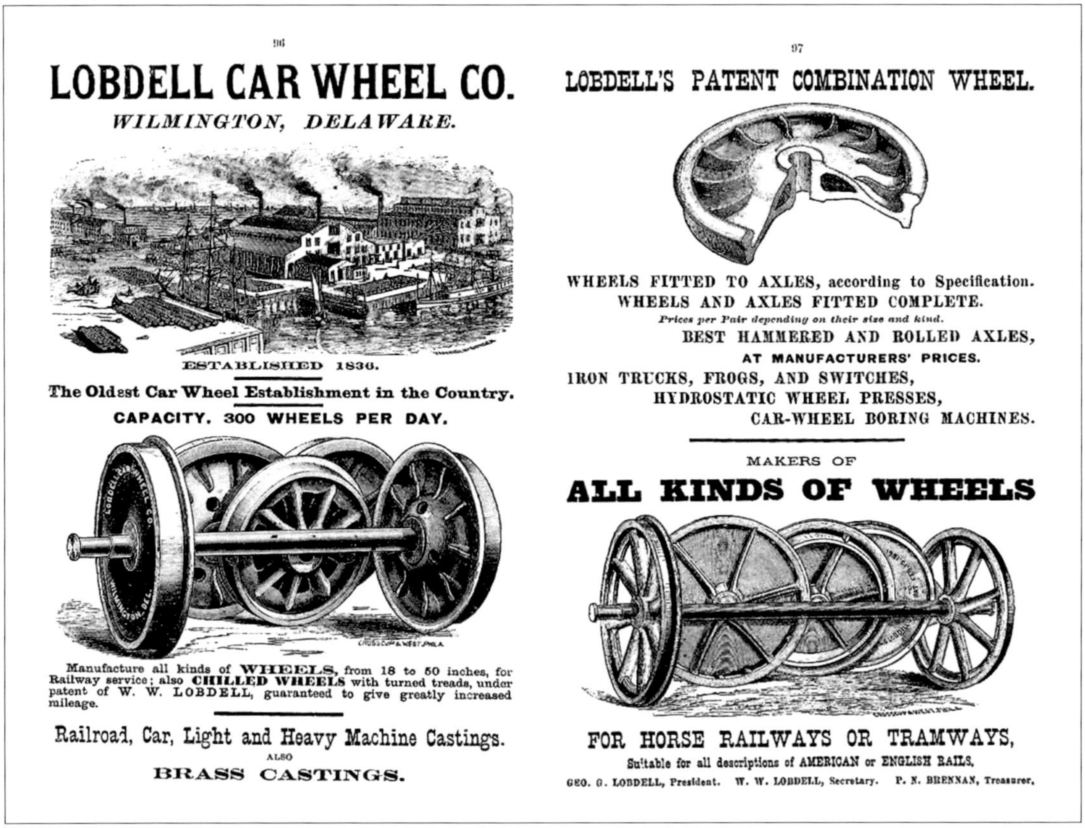

The Lobdell Car Wheel Company was organized in 1830 and by 1881 it needed a new plant to keep up with demand. The factory was built on the Christiana River in south Wilmington, giving the firm one of the largest car wheel factories in the world. In 1880 Lobdell purchased three cold-blast charcoal iron furnaces in southwestern Virginia to insure a constant supply of raw materials. The firm also manufactured chilled rolls for paper machines and flour mills, as well as chilled railroad rails.

Appendix

Railroads Built on Delmarva

Amtrak	1971
Baltimore & Ohio	1827
Baltimore and Delaware Bay Railroad	1881
Baltimore and Eastern Railroad	1923
Baltimore and Eastern Shore Railroad	1886
Baltimore, Chesapeake and Atlantic Railway	1894
Baycoast	2006
Breakwater and Frankford Railroad	03/08/1871
Cambridge and Seaford RR	1883
Cape Charles Railroad	3/24/1906
Chester and Wilmington Electric Railway	04/27/1895
Conrail	1974
Delaware and Chesapeake	03/03/1869
Delaware and Pennsylvania	02/26/1857
Delaware & Western	1877
Delaware Coast Line	1982
Delaware, Maryland, and Virginia Railroad	1883
Delmarva Central	2016
Doe Run and White Clay Creek Railroad, Corp in PA	03/24/1868
Dorcester and Delaware RR	02/06/1866
DuPont Gunpowder Factory	

Eastern Shore	1833
Eastern Shore 1975	1981
Eastern Shore Railroad 1853	1853
Elsmere and Wilmington Electric Railway Company	05/01/1895
Front and Union Street Railway	02/20/1877
Junction and Breakwater	02/13/1857
Kent County and Smyrna and Delaware Bay Railroad	09/1873
Kent County Maryland RR	1868
Kent County Railroad	03/16/1865
Landenberg Branch/B & O	
Maryland & Delaware	1977
Maryland & Delaware Seacoast	1932
Maryland and Delaware	02/13/1857
Maryland and Delaware Coast Railroad	1927
Maryland and Delaware Ship Canal Company	1880
Maryland, Delaware and Virginia	1905
New Castle & Frenchtown RR	01/16/1830
New Castle & Wilmington	1839
New Castle and Wilmington Passenger Railway	02/18/1859
New York, Philadelphia and Norfolk Railroad	1882
New York, Philadelphia and Norfolk RR Ferry Company	
Newark and Delaware City Railroad	03/29/1880
Norfolk Southern	1987
Ocean City Western Railroad	1974
Odessa and Middletown Railway	04/08/1873
Peninsula Railroad Company of Maryland	04/10/1880
Peninsula Railroad Company of Virginia	02/09/1882
Peninsular Railroad Company	1863
Penn Central	1968
Pennsylvania and Delaware Railroad	03/17/1873
Pennsylvania Railroad	1846
Philadelphia, Baltimore, and Washington Railroad	1902
Philadelphia, Wilmington and Baltimore Railroad	1836
Pomeroy and Newark Railroad	12/29/1881
Queen Anne & Kent Railroad	1856
Queen Anne's Railroad	1894
Septa	1962
Smyrna and Delaware Bay RR	02/14/1865

The Delaware Railroad Company	06/20/1836
The Gordon Heights Railway Company	05/06/1895
Virginia and Maryland	1977
Virginia Ferry Corporation	
Wicomico and Pocomoke Railroad	1848
Wilmington and Brandywine Springs Railway	04/14/1893
Wilmington and New Castle Electrical Railway	03/21/1893
Wilmington City Railroad	02/04/1864
Wilmington, New Castle and Delaware City Railway	
Wilmington and Northern	1877
Wilmington and Susquehanna Railroad	01/18/1832
Wilmington and Western Railroad	1867
Worcester and Somerset and Peninsula Railroad	
Worcester and Somerset Railroad	Aug 1871
Worcester RR	1853

Railroads That Were Chartered but Never Constructed on Delmarva

Baltimore, Chesapeake and Delaware Bay Railroad	
Cambridge to Bishop Head MD	
Christiana Railroad	04/09/1885
Clayton and Smyrna Railroad	02/07/1861
Delaware and Chester County Railroad	02/05/1867
Delaware Central Railroad	01/24/1865
Delaware City and New Castle County Railroad	03/04/1875
Delaware Terminal Railroad	05/15/1891
Delaware Western Railroad	
Delmar and Millsbourgh Railroad	03/07/1877
Dover and Bayshore Railway Company	05/07/1897
Dover and Mahon River Railroad	01/24/1865
Dover and Milford Railway	03/04/1895
Eight Street Passenger Railway	04/01/1889
Elkton and Middletown Railroad	03/28/1879
Farmers and Millers Railroad	03/11/1863
Frederica Railroad	02/19/1857
Georgetown and Delmar Railroad	02/16/1871

Georgetown and Gumbourgh Railroad	03/11/1869
Gumborough and Berlin Railroad	
Harrington, Frederica and Denton Electric Railway Company	05/03/1895
Henlopen Electric Light and Railway Company	05/01/1895
Laurel and Roaring Point Railroad	03/11/1891
Lewes and Millsbourgh Railroad	02/02/1835
Lewes Railroad and Wharf Company	02/23/1855
Lewisville Marine Railway	03/15/1871
Maryland and Woodland Beach Railway	05/28/1897
Middletown and Elkton Railroad	03/14/1871
Milford and Bayshore Railroad	03/22/1871
Mispillion and Choptank Railroad	02/17/1857
New Castle and Octorarra Railroad	02/02/1855
New Castle and Wilmington Narrow Gauge Railroad	03/29/1871
New Castle Marine Railway	02/28/1849
New Castle, Newport and Wilmington Passenger Railway	05/14/1897
New Jersey and Delaware Central Railroad	
Newark and Avondale Railroad	03/11/1867
Odessa and Middletown Narrow Gauge Railroad	04/08/1873
Queenstown and Harrington Railroad	02/26/1869
River Front Railroad	01/21/1869
Seaford and Lewes Railroad	02/26/1857
Smyrna Station and Smyrna Railroad	02/07/1861
South Side Railway Company	05/14/1897
Sussex Electric Railway Company	05/06/1895
Sussex Midland Railroad	03/26/1875
Wilmington and Brandywine Passenger Railway	04/11/1883
Wilmington and Brandywine Railroad Company	02/26/1849
Wilmington and Delaware River Railroad	02/03/1859
Wilmington and Reading Railroad Company	02/22/1877
Wilmington, Shelpot and Edgemoor Passenger Railway Company	03/17/1873